S·O·S

S·O·S

SUSTAIN

OUR

SCHOOLS

Patricia Albjerg Graham

 HILL AND WANG

A division of Farrar, Straus and Giroux

New York

Library of Congress Cataloging-in-Publication Data
Graham, Patricia Albjerg.
S.O.S. : sustain our schools / Patricia Albjerg Graham. — 1st ed.
p.   cm.
1. Education—United States—Aims and objectives. 2. Public
schools—United States. 3. Educational change—United States.
I. Title. II. Title: SOS. III. Title: Sustain our schools.
LA217.G73 1992   370'.973—dc20   91-13633 CIP

For Meg
wonderful as a child
even better as an adult

Contents

Preface

This book began with an unsuccessful trip to the library. Early in 1977 I was called for an interview with Joe Califano in Washington, D.C., to determine whether I should become the director of the National Institute of Education. Knowing little about NIE or about the federal government's role in education, I followed a strategy I had turned to often in my life, and went to the library to look up whatever had been published about NIE or, more important, about what the federal government had done or was supposed to do to improve American education. I found very little about either. On that raw winter day I would have settled for a handbook on the federal government's historical and contemporary role in education, but I could not find one.

Despite the failure of my research, I took the job, and during the ensuing two and a half years I had no time to search any more libraries. Often, during that hectic time, I wished vainly for a small volume that would explain briefly and simply what the issues were in improving American education and what the federal government could do to help.

When I returned to university teaching in 1979, I inaugurated a course on the historical role of the federal government in American education, as a means of learning something about it. In 1981 I received a grant from the Spencer Foundation to write a book on the topic. A few months later I was named dean of the Harvard Graduate School of Education, and my time for research and writing was severely curtailed. In the intervening decade I have continued to teach the course and work on the subject, but, as often happens, my understanding of the issue has changed. While I still believe the federal government has an important role to play, I also consider it imperative to involve a larger group of institutions—families, higher education, and business—in improving American education.

I am particularly grateful to H. Thomas James, president of the Spencer Foundation in 1981, and to his successor, the late Lawrence Cremin, both of whom had served as heads of schools of education, for allowing me to work on this project at a slowed pace as a consequence of my administrative duties and for understanding that my definition of the topic changed over the decade. They provided a model of foundation support for a scholar.

In the preparation of this book I have been profoundly assisted by a number of persons, particularly students at the Harvard Graduate School of Education who have participated in a course on the history of American education that I have taught in various incarnations since 1979. I am also very grateful to a number of groups around the country who have patiently listened to me talk about my evolving ideas on these subjects over the last several years and who have asked probing questions and offered wise criticism. I am especially indebted to several research assistants: Catherine Lacey and Jeanne Amster, who have worked with me on this manuscript; and Michael Fultz, Katherine Merseth, Victor W. Henningsen III, Linda Eisenmann, Roger Sharpe, and Ruben Carriedo, who aided me in earlier formulations of these issues. Several individuals have read versions of the book and commented most helpfully upon it: Derek C. Bok, Nathan Glazer, Marguerite Graham, Harold Howe II, Jerome T. Murphy, Robert Selman, and David Tatel.

Keith Whitescarver has exemplifed the best in professional collegiality as he has helped me move the manuscript from a draft to a book. Camille Smith has edited it with verve and intelligence. Arthur Rosenthal has thoughtfully encouraged me throughout the process. My colleagues in the Office of the Dean at the Harvard Graduate School of Education have watched with amusement as I have weathered the writing and editing process that is so familiar to our students, and I am grateful to them all. My husband Loren's involvement with this process has been tempered with his own vigorous editorial skills and his perpetual support. I appreciate both, but without the latter there would have been no book and not much of a life.

S·O·S

· 1 ·

No Golden Age

In September of 1955 I was twenty years old, newly married, and a recent college graduate. I did not like school. I had dropped out of high school at sixteen after discovering the volume in the school library with the state regulations revealing that you were entitled to a high school diploma after completing thirty-two units. I calculated my courses, discovered I had finished the minimum required, and showed the passage to the high school principal, who reluctantly admitted that I had fulfilled the legal requirements and sensibly told me to discuss this with my parents. I went first to the employment office, found a job at seventy-five cents an hour as a clerk-typist, accepted it, and then went home and told my parents. They were not pleased.[1]

I worked for not quite a year, saved my money, and went off to the University of Wisconsin, scared to death, as a freshman. My father got sick, and I went back home, transferred to Purdue as a sophomore, met the man who was to become my husband, finished college in two years, and married him on the day he was commissioned an ensign. As a bride in Norfolk, Virginia, I wanted a job in publishing. The newspapers would not have me. Finally, I was offered two positions, one with Smith-Douglas

Chemical Fertilizer and the other with Royster Guano, in both cases to edit their internal house organ, referred to by Royster Guano as their "poop sheet." Even I did not see my future as editing a guano poop sheet.

Reluctantly I turned to schools. Given my shortened high school and college experiences, it was clear that I felt some ambivalence about these institutions and had not wanted to spend my allotted time in them. Nonetheless, like many girls of my era, I had gotten a teacher's certificate in college, as we then explained it to ourselves, as an "insurance policy." I dragged myself down to Craddock High School, met a lovely and generous man, the principal, Mr. Booker, who talked with me about the possibility of teaching science and French, both remote from my major and minor in English and history. Gently he suggested that I might do better to inquire down the road at Deep Creek. I did, and met W. Leon Jones, the principal there, who was a bit harassed and wanted to move the guidance counselor out of the eighth-grade English and social studies classes he was teaching so that he could attend to the needs of the students. Mr. Jones offered me the counselor's four classes plus the speech/drama course, about which I knew absolutely nothing. Nonetheless, since my husband and I were in debt for our college educations, I took the job at a salary, I believe, of $2,250 for the year.

Initially I was a little disconcerted. In that year after *Brown v. Board of Education* Deep Creek was an all-white school but it was not a place of universal academic distinction or even universal high school graduation. The dropout rate was high: there were 140 in the eighth-grade class and 101 in the ninth, but only 40 seniors remained.

And then, to my astonishment, I fell in love with education, with schools, and with kids. Like many romances mine was tumultuous. My ninth-grade homeroom and my four sections of eighth-graders were determined to prove that they could best this greenhorn teacher with the funny northern accent, and in the early days they often did. I had a dead rat hurled through the door of my classroom, buckets of water dumped on the class, a gun pulled on me in the hallway, and other incidents of a type familiar to beginning teachers everywhere. By Thanksgiving, however, things had calmed down, and I no longer believed that our relationship was primarily adversarial. I was immensely helped by my neighbor in the room across the hall, Nell Casteen, who exemplified wisdom, common sense, and commitment to the children's learning found in the best experienced teachers. My debt to her is enormous.

By Christmas I was beginning to feel the pull of the developing love affair. I remember when eighth-grader Dickie read his first book, one about the Indian guide Sacajawea. He had never read a book before in his life, and he was thrilled. So was I. I remember when Wayne composed a cogent and clear essay based on investigation pursued in the library. He was proud, and I was ecstatic. I remember when Rose suddenly decided that she was no longer going to be obstreperous in class but was going to study. She did and became genuinely interested in both American history and English, discovering that academic learning was almost as compelling as playing with the boys. I was delighted.

My most traumatic adventure at Deep Creek involved not the eighth-graders or the ninth-graders in my homeroom but rather the juniors and seniors in the speech/drama class. Principal Jones informed me that since I taught the drama class, I was also expected to direct the one-act play in the inter-school competition. I was aghast. I went to the Norfolk Public Library over the weekend and read three books on how to direct a play. We had no time to order suitable playbooks for the class, so we chose the one play of which I found copies in a school closet. Called *The True in Heart*, it was set in a jail and involved the prisoners, the jailer, and the jailer's wife. It was not a work of outstanding literary merit, but it was all we had. The cast worked very hard, and we won the district competition at Princess Anne High School. We then went on to the state competition in Charlottesville, the first time that several members of the cast had been outside of Tidewater. I was nervous as I chaperoned these active young people, but they behaved beautifully and, despite the competition of large schools with well-established drama programs, won second place in the state. As we drove back to Deep Creek in my seven-year-old Chevrolet, I was enormously proud of them.

Like most love affairs, this one had its low moments too. Perhaps most poignant were the ones involving children whom we—the school and I—failed. One child in the eighth grade required services that we did not provide: she could neither read nor write and was not toilet trained. She was often the butt of her classmates' jokes, and these hurt her. A second girl who was frequently absent finally explained to me that while she would have liked to come to school regularly, her father insisted she remain with him as he moved from one hiding place to another. A few weeks later the local newspaper reported his arrest on charges of murder. A third student was repeating eighth grade for the third time, and not surprisingly this young man in a class of boys and girls was making little academic progress and creating much social disruption on the infrequent occasions when he came to school.

When school was over in June, I was hooked on schools, and I have remained so for all these years. My love affair with education, kids, and schools continues unabated. Because of this continuing romance, I have wanted to write about our children, their schools, and the help both need.

More Learning for More People

As we move to enhance the education of American children today, we must educate a much higher fraction of the population than previously to much higher levels of attainment than we have reached in the past. In short, our goal must be more learning for more people. Accomplishing this dual objective will require formidable commitments of social will, educational expertise, and financial resources. Elements of will, expertise, and financing are already in place and in some communities are adequate, but in other communities they are not. Our concern must be to sustain the communities that are educating their children well and to improve the education in other communities.

Of course, there are many good schools in America at the present time. Furthermore, we are fortunate in having many wonderful children with all the talent and motivation necessary for good education. Both such schools and such children are a joy to see, and all of us can take pride in their existence.

Our country is troubled, however, by the impediments that many children face in their transit to adulthood and that many schools face in their efforts to educate. Obstacles for children can be poverty, community disdain for education, violence in their neighborhoods, familial disorder, or an unhealthy environment. Some children flourish despite these problems, but too many do not. Obstacles for schools include community lassitude, inflexible bureaucracies, inadequate financial support, and overtired and underprepared students, teachers, and administrators. Some schools, too, do well in the face of these difficulties, and like the children who persevere, they merit our most profound congratulations and respect.

On the whole, over the years, American schools have accurately reflected the attitudes toward education in their communities. Affluent and powerful parents generally have made sure that schools in their communities provided educations that would allow their children to replicate their own status in the society. Similarly, poor parents, often without power in their communities, have also had schools that led their children to replicate their status in the society, although such replication is not what most poor parents have wanted for their children. Rather, they have sought but frequently have not gotten schools that would give their children greater opportunities than they themselves have had. Schools serving children of the poor in the United States typically have the least distinguished teachers, are the most dilapidated physically, and are profoundly encumbered by bureaucratic regulations. In short, society's sentiments, as they are expressed in education, have typically benefited the affluent and deprived the poor.

There is much clamor in America today about the present failures of our schools. There are nostalgic calls for a return to the golden age when presumably all children lived in two-parent homes where white-aproned mothers prepared milk, orange juice, and hot cereal for white-collared fathers and well-scrubbed boys and girls before the kids cheerily skipped off to the neighborhood school accompanied by their pup, Spot. At least that was the picture presented in the basal readers of the mid-twentieth century. That was also the time when Deep Creek High School was an all-white school with a 75 percent dropout rate. But such yearnings for a return to an earlier era are misguided for two reasons: there was no golden age of American schooling, and what may have been good enough before is not good enough now.

Nostalgic yearning vastly exceeds genuine reform in education. If there has ever been a subject on which it is easy to find opinion but not action, education is it. Why this reluctance to change?

Sluggish Educational Change

Currently much of the talk about educational reform in the United States focuses nearly exclusively upon the limitations of the schools. While I believe there is profound need and opportunity to improve many of our schools, I also believe that unless Americans as a people come to value both their children and their children's educations more than they currently do, efforts to improve schools alone will be but a finger in the dike against the flood of domestic malaise. Many Americans would prefer to limit the discussion of the problems of education to the failures of schools, and while that is appealing to those outside the schools because it places the burden of correcting the problems on some other institution, it is wrong both analytically and politically.

Fundamental changes in attitude and action by many segments of American society are required if education of the young in America is to improve. That is the first and most important reason why educational reform is so difficult.

Societal shifts of these dimensions are accomplished in America at evolutionary, not revolutionary, rates. Gradually we come to realize that what we have been doing educationally is not good enough, but the recognition comes sluggishly. After recognition of the need comes the attempt at action. There have been and will be many attempts to find a simple solution or "magic bullet," such as merit pay, vouchers, undefined restructuring, mentoring, or cooperative learning. But we must come finally to the conclusion that our society must strengthen its commitment to education, that the schools by themselves cannot bring about improved education for everybody.

A second reason change falters is that there have been few positive incentives for schools or school systems as a whole to improve and even fewer sanctions if they did not. School people, often principals but particularly teachers, who successfully bring about improvements in their institutions frequently find themselves exhausted by the effort, unappreciated and unsupported by the school system—and many of them then leave the schools. A poignant example is Jessica Siegel, an extraordinarily gifted teacher at Seward Park High School on the Lower East Side in New York City. Samuel Freedman describes her and her efforts in his book *Small Victories*, and he concludes regretfully that her decision to leave teaching and become a journalist is an entirely understandable one.[2] The structure of rewards and penalties for success and failure of schools and their staffs is not nearly as well developed as the one for children.

Third, the impetus to change languishes because despite the rhetorical exuberance about education, for most people it is their third or fourth priority, and the press of life makes it difficult even to attend to their first or second priority. For example, several economists, Paul Samuelson, Lester Thurow, Martin Feldstein, and Felix Rohatyn, were discussing the U.S. involve-

ment in the Middle East on a television news program recently.
Midway through their discussion of oil prices, the American
economy, and Saddam Hussein, someone mentioned education.
Dutifully each paid obeisance to its importance—even greater
than the Middle East crisis, some opined. Then they returned
to the serious business of what changes in the price of oil might
do to the U.S. economy. Given the press of other compelling
business, education with its relative absence of a crisis component recedes from the top of the public agenda.

Fourth, change comes slowly because educators have not
been forceful either about improving our schools or about building support for the efforts. With some important exceptions,
educators as a group have not emerged as architects for systemic
reform. While there are many isolated and scattered examples
of schools performing well under difficult circumstances, there
are few systems that can take pride in the academic achievement
of the bottom half of their ninth-graders. Nor are there many
systems that can point with confidence to the effectiveness and
efficiency of their operations. As American business has recently
dramatically reduced the size of middle management, are educators still confident that the growth in the number of administrators in school systems over the last several decades is entirely
appropriate? Are educators also willing to justify on the grounds
of quality of teaching the job security of experienced teachers
and the job insecurity of more recently hired ones? Until educators take broader responsibility for their efforts and shape the
public debate about how education must improve, reform will
be difficult.

Though it is distinctly unpopular to say so at the moment,
education in America has many strengths. We offer a profoundly
better school experience to our minority and our poor children
as a group than we did fifty years ago. Many American youth
benefit from a much stronger and broader curriculum, taught
in much more imaginative and compelling ways, than was true
a generation ago. The outside-of-school educational resources of
many of our communities are far more varied and more available

than they were before the communications revolutions of the late twentieth century. The finest education in the world is available in America, but not all our children manage to reap its benefits. How concerned are we—and what can we do— about those who are not succeeding? That is our conundrum.

The most powerful impetus for change in education today comes from the dissatisfaction many Americans feel with our country. A sense of unease certainly is not unique in our history, but the focus of the concern is new. Today we worry that too many Americans are either mired in or slipping into poverty; we worry that too many of our American industries are lagging in rates of productivity in comparison with those of other nations; we worry that too many Americans are ignoring or eschewing their community and civic obligations, as shown by low voter turnouts, limited political participation, expressed disenchantment with public figures; we worry that too many Americans exhibit moral passivity, seeking personal fulfillment for themselves alone rather than through building sustaining relations with friends and families, with their work, with their country, and with their spiritual commitments. In short, four problems beginning with p plague us: poverty, productivity, public participation, personal passivity. About all these matters we worry.

Schools as Social Reformers

Traditionally when we have faced national crises we have sought educational remedies, preferring to deal with the young rather than with the grownups. One hundred and fifty years ago Horace Mann promised that Massachusetts would have higher standards of morality and productivity in the Commonwealth if it created a public education system. In 1862 Justin S. Morrill promised the Congress that farm productivity and industrial growth would increase if the federal government would provide land grants to states to support instruction in agriculture and the "mechanic arts" in their colleges. During World War II government planners, fresh from the Depression experience of high rates of unemployment, envisioned a way to avoid the anticipated glut of workers in the American economy following demobilization of the troops after the war. Their solution was to send many of the veterans to college under the G.I. Bill, thus slowing their reentry into the workforce as well as providing at public expense additional education that could be used to benefit both the individuals and the society. In 1954 de jure segregation by race was declared illegal by the U.S. Supreme Court, and the institutions given the leading responsibility for implementing the decision were the public schools.

Educators, thus, are accustomed to being handed society's larger dilemmas. Over the years educators have shown themselves to be extraordinarily adept at sensing what the country really believed about an issue and adapting the educational remedy to that societal concern. For example, the social pressure for much of this century has been to reduce the dropout rate, particularly among high school students. The schools have been extremely effective in reducing that rate and in increasing the proportion of students who get high school diplomas or the equivalent GED (General Educational Development) credential. In the early years of this century less than 10 percent of American young people graduated from high school, and now more than 85 percent have either a high school diploma or a GED.[3]

The issue, however, was reducing dropout rates and raising high school graduation rates, not ensuring high levels of academic achievement. Similarly, in the press for school desegregation, the effort was to eliminate de jure segregation, not to increase the academic achievement of all children, both black and white. When there has been major societal pressure for increased academic achievement at the precollegiate level, such as that precipitated by the Soviet Union's launching of Sputnik in the fall of 1957, it has been for only a small fraction of our youth. The federal legislation that resulted from the national clamor over Sputnik, the National Defense Education Act, accurately captured the political motivation for providing better scientific training for an elite group of students who might go on to become scientists who could be more successful technically than the Soviets. Similar efforts by the National Science Foundation to improve the school mathematics and science curriculum focused upon college-bound students, not on the majority who were not intending to go to college. In short, educators have responded to social pressures accurately, providing a custody service for the many while providing a strong academic program for the few. In the past we believed that this arrangement served us reasonably well. Today we do not think so.

What is novel about our present concern is that our focus has shifted from the leaders to the workers. We are concerned about the skills of the many, not simply the skills of the few. Even though we could, perhaps, attribute our current worries to a lack of vital leadership in the society, the focus of public debate today is upon the failings of the many, not of the few. Hence, public school people, with their keen ear for the societal melody, are realizing that they are again expected to tackle a major domestic difficulty. They are appropriately concerned about the strength of their institutions and of themselves to take on what is essentially not school reform but social reform.

It is ludicrous for society to expect public schools by themselves to solve these fundamental social problems. It is also ridiculous to expect improved education, a much broader notion than schooling itself, to resolve them. Nonetheless, education, in general, and schools, in particular, can—with substantial additional supports and significant modifications in their present arrangements—make important and substantive contributions to the problems of poverty, productivity, public participation, and personal passivity. The problems, of course, feed on one another, and the educational focus must be to nurture the wit and the character of the young so that they will have the skills, attitudes, and values that will enable them to lead fulfilling and meaningful adult lives. Too many adults do not do so today, and that is bad for the country.

Mounting evidence reveals that our children are even more

likely than our adults to have difficulty achieving these skills, attitudes, and values. Therefore, the assistance of the comprehensive, tax-supported institution serving children, the public school, is sought. Poverty is significantly greater among children than among adults; productivity increases depend to some degree upon better academic skills and work habits among American workers; public participation is a value that can be fostered by education and schooling; personal passivity can be overcome by the appeal of engaging educational activities.

Schooling is a vital but limited aspect of education. Among the many agencies that educate—families, media, communities, religious, eleemosynary, and social institutions—schooling is undoubtedly much less influential than the cumulative effect of the others. Schooling's impact is considerably weakened, as well, when its message to study hard and avoid moral temptations is contradicted by what the youngster sees in the community or on TV, or even at home. Schools, however, are the only one of these institutions whose primary business is supposed to be education, as opposed to nurturant love or entertainment. Further, schools are more responsive both to public policy and to pressure than are the others. In the United States we have been reluctant to mandate and enforce child-rearing regulations, and we have for different reasons been unwilling to regulate television transmissions in a meaningful way with a view to their influence upon the young or their educational consequences. Neither have we been very effective in promoting community educational activities or in combating the abuse of drugs and alcohol. We have, however, been quite successful in building a universal school system, and hence we look to it to resolve these myriad difficulties.

American School Success

The story of American schools is a story of success—limited success, but success just the same. The schools have done an extraordinarily effective job of educating a diverse and heterogeneous population. Traditionally American schools have done quite well with healthy, well-motivated children of stable families. They have not done well—nor, for that matter, have any school systems anywhere—with unhealthy, unmotivated children without stable families. Today we have proportionally many more of the latter children in our schools and proportionally fewer of the former.

In addition, we now have significantly higher expectations for what all children need to learn than we used to have. The schools, thus, are expected to take students who are less school-oriented and teach them more. Further, they are being called upon to do this at a time when many of the able teachers, particularly women and minorities, who formerly staffed the schools have left to pursue other more rewarding vocations. The combination is not a happy one. Despite these difficulties the schools have persevered, doing well, but not well enough. As they are now being asked to shoulder the major burden of reform, they need assistance.

Many affluent and middle-class families have long recognized the importance of good schools for their children and have sought homes in communities that they believed provided such institutions. The populations of Winnetka, Scarsdale, and Alamo Heights attest to such familial decisions. Other families have made similar decisions on behalf of their children by sending them to Andover, Groton, or Dalton. Often with substantial financial effort, these families have opted for what they considered fine educations for their children, good teaching and good classmates.

While many privileged families believe in the importance of education for their children, so also do many less privileged families. For some children, school is the one structured, secure environment in their lives. In Boston nine-year-old Zakia rises at 5:30 A.M. from her bed in a welfare hotel and with her mother and three-year-old sister rides two buses in order to attend a public school, which with its free breakfast program at 8:30 A.M. prepares her for a day of study and sturdy accomplishment, an anomaly in the environment in which her family lives. Any mother who regularly rises before dawn and totes a toddler on two buses to escort her nine-year-old safely to school is one who deeply believes in education and acts on her commitment. Such efforts deserve greater support from the rest of us.[4]

Changing Expectations for Schools

Many Americans reminisce fondly about a golden age of American education. They long for the time when children were obedient, civic strife was at a minimum, and academic achievement was universal among those for whom the society was concerned. The institutions responsible for the golden age, they assert, were the schools.

Today the longing to return to the mythic golden age comes from the perceived decline in academic achievement among American high school students. Much of the current debate about educational reform in the United States focuses upon the need for higher levels of academic achievement among higher percentages of American youth. The role of schools in effecting that transformation is central, but some critics mistakenly argue that the schools alone are causes of the academic inadequacies of American youth. Schools indeed bear some of that culpability, but they share it with others: families whose interest in their children's athletic prowess is greater than their interest in their studies; employers who hire teenagers for dead-end jobs for twenty or more hours per week during the school year; communities that pay their able and effective teachers $25,000 annually and expect them to remain in teaching. In short, all of us have responsibility for the current shortcomings in academic achievement, and for creating the conditions that will make better education for everybody not just a slogan but a reality.

The goal of high levels of academic achievement for everybody, in fact, is a new one. There was no golden age in American education when either achievement or everybody was the focus of attention. Attendance, not achievement, has been a goal. High achievement for some, but not for all, has been a goal. Never in the history of American education has a high level of achievement for all our children been a seriously pursued objective for our schools. To proclaim today that we seek such universal achievement is to announce a radical new aspiration both for the schools and for our society.

The story of education in America in the twentieth century is the story of shifting expectations. Changing expectations obviously affect our sense of accomplishment. Concomitant with higher expectations for the schools, however, has come a deterioration in the lives of many children, exemplified by increased poverty, unstable families, and reckless consumerism. Children in poverty without settled families and awash in the desire for fashionable objects are not easy to educate. Further, many children are less subject than formerly to authority exerted by their parents, by other adults, or by their communities. And yet the schools of today, unlike the schools of yesterday, are expected to educate everybody to a respectable level of achievement through high school. Schools are supposed to achieve this when they are standing as the single island of compassionate efficacy in the lives of many children and of constitutional conformity in many communities.

Much of the yearning for the golden age is rooted in a wish to return to a simpler time when children were more childlike, more easily controlled, and when schools served a much smaller fraction of the young. Undoubtedly that was an easier time, particularly for those who succeeded under the old rules. For them, it was indeed a golden age; for those who did not, and there were many, it was not. Today the practices of the past are inadequate for the present and irrelevant for the future. The practices are no longer applicable because our expectations for both our children and our schools have changed so significantly in this century.

Adolescence: Longer and Longer

The principal changes in expectations for children have been concentrated in adolescence. It now begins earlier, lasts longer, and is much more confusing than it was at the beginning of the century.

Adolescence was invented, so to speak, in the twentieth century. In 1904, G. Stanley Hall published his landmark study, *Adolescence: Its Psychology and Its Relations to Physiology, Anthropology, Sociology, Sex, Crime, Religion, and Education.* Hall's greatest contribution was in popularizing the notion of a distinct and normal period in young people's lives between childhood and adulthood and the idea that this developmental phase required special attention.[5]

Hall's scholarly treatise on adolescence would not have found such a wide audience, nor would his ideas have been so influential, had there not, in fact, been some very substantial changes occurring among adolescents themselves and in the institutions that served them. Fundamentally these changes were in three domains: biology, work, and school. Largely as a consequence of better health and nutrition in the late nineteenth and early twentieth centuries, American youth were reaching physical maturity at earlier ages. For example, the average age of menarche in the United States dropped from sixteen in the middle of the nineteenth century to fourteen in the early years of the twentieth century to twelve and a half in the 1980s.[6] As the age of puberty has dropped, so also, perhaps paradoxically, have a number of the social conventions limiting intimacy between the sexes. Hence, adolescence occurs earlier among young people, just as fewer social constraints and more freedoms are being presented to them, and as schools are trying to retain them longer.

The consequence of such changes is increased sexual activity, often followed by pregnancy, which limits the teenage mother's opportunities and may result in a low-birth-weight baby at risk for normal development. Adolescent and out-of-wedlock pregnancy is not new, but it has become more widespread over the decades. During my first year of teaching in rural Virginia in 1955–56, three girls in my ninth-grade homeroom were expelled from school because they were pregnant. I was dismissed at the end of the year, too, because I was also pregnant. The three girls were not married, but I was, and my dismissal was on the grounds that a pregnant teacher provided a bad example or role model for the students. I strongly doubt that any pregnant teacher has ever been a significant influence on a teenager's likelihood of becoming pregnant. Nonetheless, schools at that time typically removed all evidence of pregnancies from the grounds. Of course, it was the young mothers and their babies who suffered when the girls were deprived of the schooling that would have helped them to support themselves. Today we are a little more enlightened: it is rare to fire a pregnant teacher; but it is also still rare, alas, to be supportive of pregnant students.

The second fundamental change that occurred simultaneously with Hall's scholarly work was the first major effort to regulate child labor. Also in 1904, the National Child Labor Committee was organized, a group that pushed for federal legislation limiting children's participation in the paid workforce. Most of the focus was upon children working in industrial settings, which were rapidly taking precedence over the predominantly rural and agricultural ones of the nineteenth century. No one seriously imagined that the federal government in Washington could regulate in a serious way a father's importuning of his son for assistance on a fishing trawler or in plowing the back forty or a mother's need for an older daughter to help with the younger children or to look after an ill relative. By 1920 the Census for the first time revealed that a majority of Americans were no longer living in rural areas but rather in communities of 2,500 or more. In such circumstances employment was more easily regulated, since it was more likely to occur in settings where wages were paid and ones in which the work of children was visible to those outside the family. Further, technology was already taking its toll of the unskilled jobs so often filled by the young, whether it were the introduction of pneumatic tubes that eliminated the need for cash boys or the telephone that obviated the need for messengers.

As urbanization became widespread, as unskilled jobs for children diminished, and as society slowly came to the conclusion that the young needed to learn more, a consensus began to develop that the answer was to keep children longer in school. In many respects this conclusion flew in the face of the biological realities, for the concentration of pubescent young people in one setting, often one they found only marginally sympathetic to their interests, was a recipe for administrative difficulties, as all who have taught or administered in junior and senior high schools can attest. Biology, however, was to be ignored, at least initially, and the needs of society, both to provide more education for the young and to keep them out of a workforce that no longer required their unskilled talents, prevailed. The proportion of seventeen-year-olds graduating from high school rose from 6 percent in 1900 to 50 percent in 1940.[7]

By the middle years of the century sociologists were discovering the significance of the adolescent peer culture and its profound concentration in the schools, isolated as they were from a strong adult culture. Urie Bronfenbrenner wrote of its various manifestations around the world and asserted that the U.S. version was especially compelling, much more so, for example, than that of either the Soviet or the Swiss society, in which adult influence seemed greater.[8]

In the affluent era after World War II, the adolescent peer culture became the focus of major advertising campaigns aimed at turning the young into consumers of products specifically oriented to them: music, clothes, motorcycles, fast foods. The products became more and more expensive: one no longer simply bought records; one needed special equipment with which to listen to them. The upright radio-phonograph in the family living room gave way to the tape recorder, to the "boom box," and to the CD player. These financial demands could no longer be met by the limited earnings from cutting lawns or babysitting, and regular part-time employment came to be much more widespread among adolescents. In earlier generations fewer teenagers had worked for money, particularly during the school year, and those who worked had typically been expected either to contribute their earnings to the family economy or to save them.

What is novel about the pattern of recent teenage employment is that it is more likely to occur during the school year, that it includes large segments of the children of the middle class and a smaller proportion of the very poor, and that the youngsters are likely to spend a large fraction of their earnings quickly. In spending their earnings immediately and not saving them the young are simply following the pattern of their elders, who are not saving much either.

At first sociologists, particularly James S. Coleman, wrote approvingly of adolescents' early move to employment, believing it preferable to keeping them isolated in the peer-driven schools. Coleman's concern with the school extended to the family when he observed that in previous generations—and, in his opinion, preferably—a father's primary exchanges with his son had been in connection with the father's activities, such as his work or his helping out at home, and therefore had been appropriate modeling examples for the son. Now, Coleman noted regretfully, the principal locales for father-son interactions were likely to be on the son's turf, at Little League games or in the Boy Scouts, both of which left the adolescents in charge with few opportunities for the grownups to provide exemplary models.[9]

Two astute observers of the educational policy scene, Eleanor Farrar McGowan and David K. Cohen, summarized the youth policy statements of the early 1970s: "According to the recent rush of reports, the solution lies in getting adolescents out of schools into work situations; or bringing work into schools so they become more like real life; or somehow combining work and schools so that labor and learning can go together. While schools used to be regarded as a better way of preparing to work, work is now seen as a better way of preparing to learn."[10] The adolescent culture had become more than the experts believed the schools could cope with, and the workplace, with what was thought to be a strong culture of its own, appeared to be a good influence on the adolescents and on the schools.

American adolescents confuse adults today. They are often difficult either singly or in groups, but they can be enchanting as well. Adults are particularly ambivalent about adolescents'

independence, unsure of how much to grant or how much will
be taken. Hence, adults at home, at school, in the workplace,
and in the society at large try to find the appropriate line between
rules and freedom or between responsibility and autonomy in
their dealings with adolescents. Over recent decades the tendency has been toward fewer rules and more autonomy. Young
people have reacted to these shifts, as well as to changes in the
economy and in their life-style expectations, by continuing to
live at home longer, often into their twenties. This development
has surprised and even dismayed many parents, but it illustrates
a paradox for American adolescents. The diminution of restric-
tions on adolescents has led them to prolong the economic dependency characteristic of childhood.

In this period of flux, clarity about appropriate parental and
adult authority regarding adolescents has become blurred. Consequently, responsibility for making decisions about both attending school and achieving academically has rested less with
adults and more with adolescents. Both groups have often found
it easier to accommodate the first requirement, attendance, than
the second, achievement. The adults and the adolescents could
make a pact on the former, but the latter demanded much more
of both than many were willing to give.

Attendance, particularly in high schools, has been the great
educational growth story of the first three-quarters of this century. For example, between 1880 and 1950 there was a fifty-fold
increase in secondary school attendance while there was a three-
fold increase in the population. The Census Bureau assures us
that if we look at an older cohort, many of whom may have
obtained their diplomas through passing high school equivalency
examinations such as the GED, as many as 86 percent are high
school graduates.[11] The phenomenal increase in high school attendance occurred early in the century, substantially ahead of
that in other industrialized nations, whose broad access to post-
elementary education came after World War II.

These figures attest to the profound changes in adolescents'
lives in the twentieth century. High school completion was a

novelty for the elite few in the early years of the century; now, at the end of the century, it is expected of everybody. Formal schooling has thus come to play a much larger and longer role in the lives of American young people.

We now expect childhood to be shorter and adolescence to be longer. The transition to adulthood is blurred by the continuation of formal schooling, and by early employment, particularly for the middle-class youths who spend and do not save their earnings, thus prolonging their financial dependency upon their families and limiting their likelihood of establishing their own homes. For many the extended period of adolescence includes sexual activity, always distracting, and for some it also includes parenthood, particularly distracting for the young mothers, many of whom do not marry and are left to rear their children either alone or while remaining in their family home, thus further complicating the divide between childhood and adulthood. The young father often is unwilling or unable to assume adult responsibilities for the child and mother, thus continuing his ambiguous and prolonged term as an adolescent.

Academic Expectations

As expectations for young people have changed, so also have expectations for schools. Americans have engaged for more than two hundred years in debate about the function of the schools: Who should attend, and for how long, and what should they study? What is the meaning of the "common" school: just for the common people? common to all? a common curriculum? Is there a different educational responsibility for future leaders than for future citizens?

In the early years of this century the president of Harvard University, Charles William Eliot, addressed a group of educators and advised them: "The teachers of the elementary school ought to sort the pupils and sort them by their evident or probable destinies."[12] Few pieces of advice from Harvard presidents have ever been so widely followed!

The "evident or probable destinies" rule had profound implications when applied by gender, by ethnicity, by race, and by social class. The development of group tests of mental ability and their widespread use after their trials by the Army during World War I (the Army Alpha and Beta) gave a patina of scientific validity to the sorting activity. Although the testers regularly cautioned against excessive reliance on the tests, they also found strong correlations between scores on the Army intelligence tests and grade in school of thirteen- and fourteen-year-old pupils. The use of the tests coincided with an excessive enthusiasm for applying scientific principles to school organization and administration in order to bring about greater "social efficiency." Hence, school people were on the lookout for justifiable ways of categorizing their pupils, and the new tests, along with studies of "retardation" (children failing to be promoted on schedule), provided evidence that children of certain ethnicities or social backgrounds predictably would be found among the achievers or the non-achievers. Thus, members of certain groups could be "attenders," as the public increasingly expected them to be, without being "achievers," which neither the public nor many educators expected most of them to be.[13]

The Russell Sage Foundation became sufficiently concerned about the failure of children to graduate from elementary schools in the early years of the century that it undertook a study, led by Leonard P. Ayres, to document the matter. Among city schools, then thought to be the best in the United States, Ayres found in 1908 that for each 1,000 pupils entering the first grade only 263 reached the eighth grade and a bare 56 reached the fourth year of high school. In less urban North Carolina the figures were substantially worse: only 139 of the entering 1,000 reached the seventh grade and only two the fourth year of high school. Ayres, a man much given to counting and categories, also noted that students of varying national origins in the New York City schools had different rates of retardation (German, 16 percent; American, 19 percent; Mixed, 19 percent; Russian, 23 percent; English, 24 percent; Irish, 29 percent; Italian, 36 percent), but he failed to tie these patterns either to how recently these families had immigrated or to their social class in the United States, both historically excellent predictors of school achievement.[14]

The existence of these different ethnic examples of success in school attracted substantial attention in the following decade and profound criticism subsequently. The *prima facie* case for the intellectual superiority of some ethnic groups over others was made most forcefully by Carl C. Brigham, an assistant professor of psychology at Princeton University, who in 1922 published a volume with a foreword by Robert Yerkes, the father of the Army intelligence tests. Brigham analyzed the results of the Army tests, under the title *A Study of American Intelligence*, and emphasized the varied scores by ethnicity. He found, for example, that if one ranked scores of foreign-born whites by country of birth, the English, Scots, Dutch, Germans, and Danes led, and the Turks, Greeks, Russians, Italians, and Poles trailed. U.S.-born whites ranked between the Germans and the Danes. In an age of scientism such results were taken seriously by some otherwise well-informed persons.[15]

As keeping these apparently widely varied ethnic groups in school became the issue, the response of the schools was to undertake significant changes in the curriculum. Most of the changes were efforts to "water down" the curriculum so that it could be learned by those the schools had concluded—on the basis of either their "evident or probable destiny," their achievement to date, their attitudes, or some combination of these—to be unlikely to prosper in the traditional course of studies. Thus came the vocational curriculum, the general curriculum, and tracking, all efforts to tailor instruction to children's seeming abilities.

How valuable was the curriculum that the children were learning? Certainly the many studies that have evaluated vocational education have found no evidence that completion of vocational studies has enhanced students' long-term employment. Nor is there any evidence that the learning provided by the alternative to the traditional curriculum was deemed equivalently valuable by the society. In fact, the shortcomings of American youths' academic achievement are not primarily those of the college preparatory group, who continue to receive usually rigorous and comprehensive instruction, but those of students in the "general" or vocational tracks. The "general" track did not even exist on a broad scale until the second half of the century.

Just as there was no golden age of Dicks and Janes skipping merrily off to school, so also there was no golden age when all students mastered an academic curriculum. Mostly, Americans did not care. There were a few lonely dissenting voices, such as Thomas Briggs, a professor at Teachers College, Columbia, who lamented in 1930 that "the authorities have made no serious efforts to formulate for secondary schools a curriculum which promises maximum good to the supporting state." He added: "The second count of the indictment would be that there has been no respectable achievement even in the subjects offered in the secondary school curricula." Briggs then cited several examples: in a select group of entering university freshmen, only half were able to find the value of b when given the equation $by = 2$; half the students who had completed a year of American history in high school failed to identify the Monroe Doctrine; and "only 29 percent of the freshmen boys and 37 percent of the freshmen girls at Indiana University could give the title of the chapter or formulate in any terms the chief problem discussed by the author" in a passage of English prose that they had had two days to study.[16] At the time, nationally, less than 30 percent were graduating from high school and just over 10 percent were attending college. Such results indicate that high school graduation even then did not necessarily mean academic achievement.

Achievement means more than explaining $by = 2$. Rather, it is the attainment of a set of skills, knowledge, and values that encourage one to learn on one's own, to participate fully in the society, and to be a competent employee. Currently we have grave concerns about all three of these qualifications for many in our population. Naively, perhaps, we attribute these difficulties to failures in school achievement. Alternatively and more wisely, we might point to a number of other societal forces, more abstract and therefore less easily identifiable than schools, to blame for these failings. A materialistic culture that rewards financial success and does not reward learning is not one in which schooling is likely to be popular. Nonetheless, inadequate academic achievement has again become a matter of national concern.

Has Achievement Declined?

During the 1970s several authors presented complaints about children's academic performance relative to that of their parents' generation. These augmented a litany of laments that had begun in the 1950s but had not then fallen on fertile soil.[17] Twenty-five years later, however, the soil was fertilized, moist, plowed, and ready to nurture the critics. The most lurid of these, Paul Copperman and Frank Armbruster, attributed the drop in academic performance to America's failure in the 1960s to maintain standards and rigor and then to the reflection of society's values in the schools in the open education movement. Copperman was cited, apparently approvingly, in the 1983 report of the National Commission on Excellence in Education, *A Nation at Risk*, giving his work a spurious legitimacy.[18]

Any responsible commentator would agree that more learning for more children would be desirable and that schools should function so as to make such learning more likely to occur. A different question, however, was whether schools had previously provided such widespread learning for all. The public relations argument was that such high standards had previously been in place and in force for all students, and that recently—in the decades of the 1960s and the 1970s—they had dropped. The simplistic line was that we simply needed to return to the good old days. A closer examination revealed that even the good old days had had lapses in literacy.

More responsible expressions of concern included a panel organized by the College Entrance Examination Board and chaired by Willard Wirtz, which released *On Further Examination*, an effort to explain why the Scholastic Aptitude Test (SAT) average scores had declined since 1963.[19] During this same period the average scores on the College Board's *achievement* tests had increased, but public attention focused on the SATs, in part because more students took them and because they appeared simpler to understand. In fact, the word "aptitude" in the tests' title was a misnomer; the tests did not purport to measure fundamental aptitude but rather the likelihood of a student's academic success in the freshman year of college. While freshman grades are in some degree related to student ability, they are affected by many other factors (amount of studying, for example). The College Board has regularly maintained that high school grades in combination with SAT scores provide greater predictive validity than the SATs alone, but the SAT scores, with their seeming precision as a marker of American adolescents' intelligence, captured the public's imagination. It seemed so easy to assume that American high school seniors were getting either dumber or smarter by watching whether the SAT scores went up or down. It was easy, but it was also false.

As Harold Stevenson and others doing cross-national studies of educational achievement have observed, Americans have a near obsession with ability as a determinant of scholastic achievement, while other societies believe, as Americans do in other domains, that hard work is at least as important as ability.[20] We seem to believe that if a child does not have an "aptitude" for mathematics or whatever subject, then the child cannot learn it. Other nations believe the child just needs to study harder. Our attitude toward athletics incorporates the mix of ability and hard work; no outstanding athlete attributes his or her performance to ability or practice alone but rather to a combination of the two. So it should be with academic performance.

The Wirtz panel's conclusion was that two-thirds or three-fourths of the drop in the scores between 1963 and 1970 could be attributed to the increase in the numbers of students from disadvantaged backgrounds, who tend to be low scorers, taking the test. In the period from 1970 to 1977, however, only one-quarter of the decline, in the panel's view, could be assigned to the new test-takers. Responsibility for the rest of the decline rested with diminished academic rigor in the school curriculum, which reflected less societal and familial support for serious academic learning. Special credit was also given to television for adversely occupying children's time. In the end, however, the panel observed that "there has been an apparent marked diminution in young people's learning motivation" and then concluded, "it is perhaps most significant of all that during the past ten years [1967–1977] the curve of the SAT scores has followed very closely the curve of the entire nation's spirits and self-esteem and sense of purpose."[21]

Wirtz and his colleagues were raising the same issue in a thoughtful, responsible fashion that Copperman and Armbruster were doing in a flashier mode, namely that what the society thought about itself influenced enormously the way in which it educated its children. In an era with a preference for quantifiable answers to complex questions, scholars have found it very difficult to provide explanations for such evanescent notions as a generation's collective motivation for learning or a nation's spirit, self-esteem, or sense of purpose. Yet it is in those arenas where the explanations for student achievement lie.

The efforts to get systematic, accurate data on students' learning in the past are confounded by many methodological problems. Consequently most serious scholars have tried to limit comparisons between past and present to issues of reading performance or crude literacy. The evidence for determining how much children in a particular period could read is typically taken from standardized tests of reading ability given to schoolchildren. The methodological difficulties of getting equivalent scores are enormous. For example, in one of the most detailed of the "then and now" studies, Roger Farr and his colleagues at Indiana University, while tentatively finding the "now" students better readers than the "then" students, summarized their findings as follows: "Our most positive conclusion is that it is extremely difficult for anyone interested in evaluating trends in literacy to obtain adequate data."[22]

The most thorough and thoughtful of the historical analyses of student achievement to date, by Lawrence C. Stedman and Carl F. Kaestle, reaches essentially the same conclusion after a careful look at the varied studies, undertaken by test manufacturers, by the Congressional Budget Office, and by other researchers, of changes in test scores, principally in reading, over the years. The authors sum up: "Our main conclusions . . . are that the data is sketchy, the research is shaky, and the trends are murky . . . Through the haze we squint, and we venture the conclusion that there probably has not been much of a decline in reading ability at a given educational level during the twentieth century, even during the controversial 1970s."[23]

The closest thing we have in the United States to a national test of academic achievement is the National Assessment of Educational Progress. Tests are given every few years to a sample of nine-, thirteen-, and seventeen-year-olds enrolled in U.S. schools. Students are tested in reading, writing, mathematics, and science. In 1988 they were also tested in geography.

The results of twenty years of NAEP testing are generally positive, revealing higher scores in recent tests than in earlier ones except for science. These changes appear to be more characteristic of younger children than of adolescents. Incidentally, these elementary students are much more likely to be beneficiaries of the Elementary and Secondary Education Act Title I (now Chapter I) services than are high school students. Minority children have also shown greater gains than whites, although minority students as a group still have substantially lower scores.

In simplest terms, then, student achievement, insofar as we can measure it by tests, has not declined dramatically in the United States. It may even have improved a little. Yet Americans do have reason to be troubled by the current academic achievement of their young. On one set of testing measures, albeit not ones that span decades, American students do badly. These are comparisons with students in other industrialized countries. On such tests U.S. youngsters trail those of Japan and most Western European nations. (There are no data on either of the other two large heterogeneous societies, the Soviet Union and China.) Americans find it upsetting to rank tenth internationally on a measure of mathematical proficiency. President Bush has announced that we will be first by the end of the decade, but his advisors do not have a clear idea of how to achieve that goal. But, as one of them observed privately, "What did you expect us to say, that we'd be eighth by the year 2000?"

Currently in the United States there are many critics of standardized testing.[24] Many believe that the tests create a linguistic screen through which a person's knowledge must pass before it can be credited to the individual. Hence, one's command of language determines unfairly what one may know about another subject. Howard Gardner and Dennie Wolf are leading groups that are exploring alternative forms of assessment that minimize the screen and attempt to ascertain what a student knows more directly. They are exploring the use of portfolios of accumulated work, videotapes of performances, as well as other means of demonstrating what students can do, not just what answers they can give to multiple-choice questions.[25] The Educational Testing Service is investing heavily in alternative modes of assessment and has already achieved new kinds of performance tests in some of its smaller examinations, for example the one for architects' licensing.

These investigations of achievement, as I have said, reflect a novel development, widespread concern among both educators and the public about the academic achievement of all Americans.[26] The novelty is the concern for achievement for all. The profound dissatisfaction expressed by so many Americans about our children's academic achievement has come at a time when, in fact, it is probably a little higher than it was in the past. This occurrence dramatically demonstrates the primary change in expectations for the schools: more learning for more people.

The Schools and Social Justice

The other fundamental change in expectations for the schools lies in their role, assigned chiefly by the courts utilizing the equal protection clause in the Fourteenth Amendment to the Constitution, in increasing social justice in America. At first, the issue was desegregation of institutions that previously had been limited to one race. The original case that established segregated facilities by law, *Plessy v. Ferguson* in 1896, had nothing to do with education. Rather, it condoned railroads' designation of separate seating for blacks and whites in the South. After World War I a number of cases attempting to challenge the legality of segregation began to make their way through the courts. Soon education became the focus, with a case involving a black man's efforts to attend the University of Missouri Law School, then an all-white institution. In *Missouri ex rel. Gaines v. Canada* in 1938 the Supreme Court decision hinted that a reversal of the separate but equal doctrine might come. The early desegregation cases involving education had focused on the inequality between institutions provided for blacks and whites, but gradually the central issue became the legality of separateness itself.

At the initiation of the minority community, the NAACP Legal and Educational Defense Fund pushed the schools to lead the society in ensuring citizens their constitutional rights. Eventually the NAACP lawyers, led by Thurgood Marshall, argued that educations could never be equal if they were separate. The Supreme Court agreed in 1954 in its unanimous decision in *Brown v. Board of Education*: "We conclude that in the field of public education the doctrine of 'separate but equal' has no place. Separate educational facilities are inherently unequal."

In the many education cases since *Brown*, the coalition of civil rights groups has worked to reveal evidence of continuing segregation within school systems and has sought remedies to eliminate those inequalities. School boards throughout the nation have recognized that they are leading the fight for social justice in America. Initially, only some accepted that role willingly, although in the last several years city boards have become advocates for their children, mostly minority and poor, and several have challenged state governments on issues of financial equity. Meanwhile, many cities have been deserted by their affluent business, professional, and civic leaders, who often have moved their children out of the public schools or their entire families to more socially, economically, and racially homogeneous communities. This move to suburbia began in the 1940s, long before the courts ordered the desegregation of urban schools, and has continued unabated. It has left the public schools in the nation's largest cities with student populations that are predominantly minority and poor, heightening the desegregation issue.[27]

Schools have a difficult time ensuring equal protection of the law for children beset by poverty or racial discrimination or both. It is unrealistic to rely on city schools alone to provide educations for children of the poor equal to those provided by schools, families, and communities together to children in more privileged communities. Recent cases in Missouri, Wisconsin, and elsewhere, organized by coalitions of civil rights groups and often joined by city school boards, have pressed to overcome the poverty and racial isolation within cities and to include suburban communities with their wealthier and whiter families in desegregation plans.

The Supreme Court decision in the *Brown* case in 1954 did not promise higher test scores for black children. Rather, it said that the government could not require children of different races to attend separate schools because such a requirement violated the constitutional provision of equal protection under the laws. In the intervening years, especially after *Milliken v. Bradley II* in 1977, this has been interpreted to mean that the quality of education provided to black and white children by the schools

must be equal. How the schools can compensate for the difficulties that minority and poor children encounter in their families and communities has not been resolved either by the courts,
the educators, or the public.

The dilemma faced by school people in the last quarter of
the twentieth century is how to meet the two new expectations
that have been placed upon them: improving academic achievement for all students and increasing social justice through the
schools. School people have been asked to do with youth what
the society as a whole has been unable or unwilling to do with
adults. The inadequacies of the American workforce are to be
corrected by better schooling, and the injustices of American
society are to be alleviated by integration of the schools.

As school systems have struggled to attain these twin goals,
some have failed, but many have succeeded. The initial efforts
at desegregation, from Little Rock in 1957 to Boston in 1974,
illustrate how difficult the educators' task has been when leaders
in their local communities have opposed the Supreme Court
decision. But the longer-term examples of steadily rising minority achievement and of peaceful and productive integrated
schools show that educators have been able to surmount those
difficulties. For example, the previously all-white high school in
which I began teaching in 1955 is now 48 percent black with a
dramatically reduced dropout rate. The Chesapeake School System, of which it is a part, now issues a "warranty" on its diplomas,
testifying that its holders meet standards of achievement consistent with high school completion. If an employer hires a graduate who does not meet those standards, the employer can return
the graduate to the high school for remediation free of charge.
This is a concrete, unheralded example of a system that has
improved in both academic achievement and social justice.
There are many similar examples scattered throughout the
United States, but they are not nearly as visible as the well-
publicized and tragic cases of school systems in our largest cities
that have not yet met those goals.

In addition to the issue of desegregation of the races, the

pressure for social justice came to focus on other inequities as well: on lack of access for girls to activities dominated by boys, on isolation of handicapped children, on the problems faced by non-English-speaking children in English-speaking classrooms, and on the lower academic performance of poor children.

The reform strategy was one of legal intervention when the coalition of civil rights groups believed the state and local authorities were failing to provide equally for the educations of American children. Sometimes federal funds were available to help achieve this aim (Emergency School Assistance Act funds were allocated to assist in desegregating school districts), and sometimes legislative and regulatory pressure was applied (Public Law 94-142 required individual education plans for handicapped youngsters, but few additional funds were provided for either developing or implementing those). Federal and state officials worked with the civil rights groups in varying degrees, from intensely adversarial relationships in the Reagan years to much more cooperative ones in the Carter administration.

The federal impact has been great for two principal reasons. First, to avoid the institutional migraines that would result from a failure to comply with procedures assigned by the courts or by state or federal programs, many school officials spent valuable time seeking the exceedingly narrow and obscure path through the forest of regulations and consistent with community sentiment. Second, the regulations and appropriations represented to some extent manifestations of national purpose in education. There was never total agreement about national educational goals, or even articulation of them, but, aided by Supreme Court decisions, a consensus gradually began to develop regarding the illegality of de jure segregation of the races in public schools, the unequal treatment of women, and the isolation of the handicapped. Less clarity was reached about bilingual education: some favored "maintenance" of the family language and some wanted "transition" to English, and no one knew how to do either well with all children.

The impact of the civil rights movement on access and opportunity was substantial, but the early emphasis among both civil rights activists and the government was on issues of process, not on issues of achievement. Initially many believed that it was simply necessary for children of all races to attend the same schools in order to get the same education. Over the years both the activists and the educators have learned that simple placement in the same building does not inevitably bring equivalent learning to the child of poverty and the child of professionals. But at the height of the civil rights movement in the 1960s, few voices called in the educational wilderness demanding universal, rigorous academic achievement.

The vast majority of school superintendents, school board members, and professors at prestigious schools of education trailed the civil rights groups, the courts, and the governmental regulators on these issues throughout the 1950s, the 1960s, and into the 1970s. Left to their own devices, few in those years would have ranked equal educational opportunity as a pressing educational issue. The ranks of educational leaders did not include many minority persons or women, and most were not deeply concerned about opportunities for either of these groups of citizens. These educators did not enjoy being first told, and then forced, to change their ways.

The educational leaders had to mend their ways, and so did their staffs, many of whom, like the leaders, had lacked both a commitment to the education of these new populations and the expertise to educate them effectively. Integration of the racial minorities was the hardest of the goals to achieve, in part because racism runs deep in American psyches, in part because issues of race were often confounded with problems of class, and in part because there were very few Blacks, Hispanics, Asians, or Native Americans in positions of educational responsibility. Equal educational access for girls came more easily than equality for women professionals, since the girls could be thought of as daughters, while the latter provided the challenge of wives and competitors. Mainstreaming the physically handicapped in many ways was the easiest of the goals to meet because the constituency supporting the handicapped cut across all social and economic classes. Many prominent persons have a member of their family who is handicapped. Further, most physical handicaps were quite definable, unlike emotional or mental ones, and were more likely to prompt pity than rage or annoyance. Who could blame a child for being deaf or blind? Blaming seemed easier when the female was pushy or the black was uppity. Yet equal educational opportunity required that all these groups be given a fair chance to succeed.

Sensible school people, of course, have long recognized that their institutions are not perfect. But the burden of being expected to solve social problems as well as educational ones, the dilemma of meeting court-defined standards while also satisfying their local communities, and the constant gap between expectations and the resources—fiscal and political—provided to fulfill them can discourage even the most dedicated educators. Many have stayed in the schools, trying to improve them; others have simply stayed. Still others, many of them highly talented and motivated, have left the schools, either utterly disheartened by the experience or committed to improving education in another venue.

In the summer of 1978 I spent nearly a month touring China with fellow Americans in a delegation known as "Local Education Leaders." Most of my colleagues were school superintendents; all the superintendents were men, and all but one of them were white. They had served such cities as Dallas, New Orleans, Atlanta, Portland, Sacramento, Austin, Columbus, and Milton, Massachusetts. To a man they understood, five years before publication of *A Nation at Risk*, that their schools were in trouble, that their leadership was threatened by the criticism of the schools, and that achievement for poor and minority children was a vital goal for their systems. Today not one of them is still a superintendent, although several are still in the field of education.

Many talented persons simply do not want to put up with the constant attack and limited support that a school superin-

tendent today faces. Turnover among the nation's one hundred
largest districts is so high that nearly two-thirds have superintendents with less than five years in their position. Average
tenure for urban superintendents is now down to two and one-
half years.[28] Teachers, particularly ones with other vocational
opportunities such as math and science specialists, also leave
with regularity, including some of the most gifted and committed. Estimates vary by subject specialization and race, but approximately half of all beginning teachers leave the schools by
their fifth year of teaching.[29] Only a rare individual can thrive
in a professional lifetime of unremitting criticism, even when
doing work that is of fundamental significance to the society.

During the Carter administration David Tatel served as the
head of the Office of Civil Rights and vigorously pushed school
districts and states to follow the law by abolishing racial segregation in their schools and colleges. Inevitably he found school
and college administrators concerned about this outside inter-
ference in their affairs. In New York, senior administrators jus-
tified tracking in the schools on the grounds that teaching
heterogeneous classes was too demanding for the skills of the
New York City teachers. In Chicago, administrators and the
editorial board of the leading newspaper agreed that if Tatel's
pressure for desegregation led to the departure of one single
white family from the city of Chicago, then they would oppose
it—and they did. Neither case showed the educators, in all cases
white men, to be strongly interested in increasing either the
educational opportunity or the academic achievement of their
predominantly minority student populations.

Both the New York and the Chicago schools have now been
headed by persons of color for the last several superintendents,
and while these individuals have expressed deep concern about
minority student achievement, their pupils are not yet demonstrating academic mastery. Having high expectations for minority achievement, then, is a necessary but not sufficient
condition for attaining it.

Thus, by the last decade in the twentieth century the shift

in expectations for the schools has come to embrace two appropriate but difficult goals: academic achievement and social justice. In our meandering fashion we Americans are coming to recognize that our future depends on educating everybody well. A heavy burden has been placed upon the schools in the last half-century to bring children of the poor and of racial and ethnic minorities into fuller participation in America than has been possible for most of their parents. Reluctantly, hesitantly, educators and the public have come to understand that if such fundamental integration is to occur, then these young people must exhibit the skills and attitudes the society values. The schools are now being asked to provide such young citizens.

These enormous demands on the schools come at a time when poverty undermines the health and motivation of more and more of our children, and when economic, sexual, and community pressures upon adolescents contradict the schools' efforts to educate them. The beleaguered schools cannot meet these demands alone. Attainment of the goal of educating everybody well will require a coalition of forces collaborating well into the twenty-first century. Families, communities, government, higher education, and business will all need to help. Will they be willing, and will they be effective? Concretely, what should they do? These are the issues for the following chapters.

· 2 ·

Families

My grandparents were Danes who settled in western Minnesota with their nine children in the late nineteenth century. They became successful farmers and urged their children to do the same. One daughter moved to Montana when she married, but the others stayed in the county—except for my father. Alone among the children he had a decisive falling-out with his father, and the issue was education. My grandfather believed that the American public schools, eight years maximum, were useful as a place to learn English and to acquire rudimentary skills. After that, one returned to the farm to work. Further schooling in his view was damaging both to the work ethic and to the values of the family.

My grandfather was a shrewd man, and he understood that further schooling would be likely to have a cosmopolitan influence that would be at variance with the values that he held himself and that he wanted his children to share. Schooling beyond the eighth grade provided more options for adulthood than farming near Underwood or carpentry in Fergus Falls. As patriarch of the Albjerg clan, my grandfather wished his children and grandchildren to be nearby, for both economic and personal reasons. If his children had more schooling, he believed, then they would be more likely to leave. He was absolutely right. The autumn my father was sixteen he began teaching rural school after having completed the eighth grade in the spring. This decision caused the break with his father, and he never lived at home again. His father understood that he would not stay down on the farm after he had seen—in this case, not Paris but Battle Lake.

Recently three of my Harvard colleagues presented educational biographies to a gathering at the Harvard Graduate School of Education. The first, Israel Scheffler, recounted the profound support his parents, Romanian Jews recently arrived in the United States, gave him to pursue his education, though there was uncertainty in the family about whether it should be the secular experience provided by New York City institutions or the religious one provided by Jewish institutions. The second, Sara Lawrence Lightfoot, read from her biography of her mother, the psychiatrist Margaret Lawrence, revealing the extraordinary efforts of Margaret's parents, aunts, and other relatives to support her in the black schools of Mississippi and then to send her to New York City for high school, where she acquired the education that allowed her to attend Cornell and subsequently medical school at Columbia University. Finally, Sissela Bok told how her mother, the Nobel Peace Prize winner Alva Myrdal, found support for her schooling beyond the elementary grades in rural Sweden not from her parents, who opposed it, but from the gangly young man who came hiking through her parents' farm and who later became her husband, Gunnar Myrdal. He became a distinguished social scientist, described the race situation in the United States as the American Dilemma in 1944, and also won a Nobel Prize, the 1974 Nobel Prize in Economic Sciences. In short, all of these extraordinary individuals received critical support for their educations from someone close to them: parents, older relatives, lovers. Few of us are successful auto-didacts. Most of us need powerful support from our families or from someone we admire in order to persevere in our educations. Ideally that support should come from our communities as well.[1]

American Anti-Intellectualism

Many Americans are ambivalent about academic achievement. While most see diplomas as useful and success as desirable, only some see academic achievement as crucial to either. Some families have rightly feared, as my grandfather did, that formal schooling would cause ruptures with their children, and some have felt uncertain about the value of extended education or worried that excessive bookishness was not good for children. Today most families strongly support elementary education for their children, and most believe that a high school diploma—if not an education—is highly desirable. College attendance is now within the reach of the majority of young people, but many families consider college a place that provides the ticket to subsequent economic success, not a place of learning.

This ambivalence forms the core of the dilemma of how to involve families more deeply in the education of their children. The attitudes of my Danish grandfather or Alva Myrdal's family are replicated in many late-twentieth-century American homes and are much more common than those of Margaret Lawrence's relatives who helped her or the parents who encouraged Israel Scheffler. Children quickly grasp familial attitudes, and while some youngsters may resist as Alva and my father did, many will simply accommodate to their family's views. And these views are often consistent with their own: academic achievement requires hard work, and many youngsters would prefer to avoid the effort and are supported explicitly or implicitly by their families in this avoidance. The residual anti-intellectualism of Americans, about which Richard Hofstadter wrote so poignantly a generation ago, remains with us.[2] In this regard Americans are very different from the prototypical Japanese family, who insist that their children study hard and who enhance and abet their offspring's academic efforts.

The universal usurper of children's time is television. Estimates vary but generally children seem to average about three hours daily in front of the set. Younger children watch more than older ones, and poor children more than affluent ones. Further, schoolchildren increased their hours of watching during the 1980s. As many families now have more than one television set, children increasingly choose programs for themselves and watch them alone without the mediating guidance and commentary of adults. While there are certainly some fine television programs available, such as the landmark Children's Television Workshop productions of *Sesame Street, Electric Company*, or *Three, Two, One, Contact!*, much of what the children watch is drivel. Their families watch it too, another indication of the anti-intellectual bias in many American families. For most children television takes the place of either reading books, playing outdoors, or participating in activities that draw more profoundly upon their imaginations than does TV.[3]

Most of all, television isolates children from their families. Time previously spent in family conversation, chores, games, or other shared pursuits is now often usurped by television (although some authors argue that adolescents' TV viewing is not nearly as deleterious for them, their family relationships, or their studies, as their listening to music—presumably rock—is).[4] The family's fundamental role of nurturing the young is thus diminished, and that is costly indeed for the child, who now learns about the world vicariously through television plots rather than directly through family interaction and activities.

The Financial Crunch

The policy process in the United States has never been very good at regulating how families rear their children. Some other nations consider it appropriate to devise government policies that significantly influence the upbringing of the next generation, arguing that the young are the nation's future. I recall a conversation more than a decade ago in Jerusalem with a leading

Israeli educator, who looked at me in astonishment when I told him that the U.S. government agency I then headed, the National Institute of Education, did not believe it should (or could) mandate good child care practices that we had identified and tested through research. We thought U.S. families should know about them but not be required to follow them. That was not the view of my Israeli colleague, who maintained that if government knew what ought to be done, it ought to insist that the public do it. I replied that we had a different tradition in the United States.

That tradition of allowing families to rear their children in ways that seem best to the families, not to the government, is one that we appropriately cherish. Yet, ironically, we often allow the establishment of government policies that make it extremely difficult for families to rear their children as well as they would like. This is particularly true for the parents who feel a financial pinch. While some may feel the pinch in order to buy a Bronco instead of a Ford Escort, many are indeed scrimping to give their children greater opportunities. The majority correctly sense that if they lived in a better neighborhood—by which they mean one that is safer, has good schools, has recreational and cultural programs for children, and, above all, is populated with adults who have become successful in legitimate endeavors—then their children would have a better chance in life.

Some suburban communities have built their entire reputations as desirable places to live on the quality of their schools. "Good schools attract a good class of people," the realtors assert. This slogan was especially compelling in the years immediately after World War II, when the birth rate rose to new heights for the twentieth century and when the federal government subsidized suburbanization through its highway and mortgage programs. Today the rhetoric is more likely to focus upon the dangers of the city than upon the benefits of suburbia.

Realtors and the rest of us recognize that the family and the community are closely intertwined in a child's life, since the child, unlike an employed parent, generally remains in the community throughout the day. Hence, the axis of home and community powerfully orients the child, and it is not always supportive of the third principal institution in the child's life, school.

Today children live disproportionately in families that do not have free choice among communities because they are poor. These families feel not a financial pinch but a financial crunch. The fraction of youthful poor has been increasing during the past decade, while poverty among the elderly has been decreasing. Nearly one-quarter of all U.S. children and almost half of U.S. black children under age six live in poverty.[5] Many poor children grow up in families that feel alienated from the schools. Poor parents who do value education may not be sure how to help their kids achieve in school—or may be too overwhelmed by daily responsibilities to meet with their child's teacher or to help the child with homework in the evenings. Many of the communities they live in have few resident adults who have succeeded through education; in fact, financial success in some neighborhoods is limited to those engaged in illicit and illegal activities, hardly an advertisement for education.

Only a minority of children now live in homes in which a parent (almost always a mother) is there full time caring for them. By 1995, the estimates are that two-thirds of children under six and three-quarters of school-age children will have mothers employed outside the home. The comparable figures for 1970 were 29 percent of children under six and 43 percent of school-age children.[6]

The principal reason these mothers are employed outside the home is that they need the money. Only a minuscule proportion are in high-paying jobs and have full-time nannies in residence looking after the children. Women, whose salaries are still only 70 percent of men's, are either supplementing the family income in order to remain in the middle or working class or providing the primary or sole income for themselves and their children. As mid-level and blue-collar salaries have declined in real dollar terms during the 1980s, many families have managed to maintain their standard of living or some approximation of it by having the wife work outside the home. A husband working full time at the minimum wage with a wife and one child can no longer provide an income that will raise his family above the poverty line. Even men substantially above the minimum wage have seen their earnings decline; the median hourly earnings of men in the age group twenty-five to thirty-four, measured in constant 1985 dollars, fell from $10.17 in 1973 to $8.85 in 1987.[7]

Hence, the solution in many families is for the wife to seek paid employment as well. Even so, family income for the poorest 20 percent of the population has fallen by 17.8 percent since 1969, with the bulk of this decline taking place during the 1980s. For the richest 20 percent of the population family income has risen nearly 10 percent since 1969, with most of this increase also occurring in the 1980s. Indeed, aggregate family income during the 1980s revealed losses for those in the bottom 80 percent and gains for the top 20 percent. The gains were greatest for the top 5 percent, whose average income rose a substantial 34 percent. The gains were so large that the overall percentage change for the population as a whole was a gain of 8.9 percent, which obscured the fact that the majority were losing ground.[8]

These figures on shifts in income tell only part of the tale about changes in family life. The shift in the psychological balance in families can be enormous. When a husband's decline in real earnings and his dim future prospects make it necessary for his wife to be employed outside the home, usually at a lower wage than her husband, the effect can be devastating to family stability and consequently to child-rearing. When money is easy and the future hopeful, inevitable stresses that occur in families can often be overcome. When bills are mounting and the years ahead look bleak, such frustrations are more likely to become overwhelming. Even if the couple does not divorce, as happens now with about half of first marriages, relaxed, supportive family life often declines as work pressures for both parents mount.[9] Many parents do not live near older relatives who can assist them. Only about 5 percent of American children now see a

grandparent regularly, a dramatic drop from previous generations. For single parents, most of whom are women, the burdens
of low income, household duties, and child care responsibilities
are heavy. The proportion of all American families headed by a
single parent has doubled in the past twenty years, from nearly
12 percent in 1970 to over 24 percent in 1987. Of black children,
54.5 percent live in single-parent homes. [10]

The issue is not that these children are loved less than children in earlier generations; these families generally love their
children deeply. But in circumstances of poverty it is extraordinarily difficult to find the additional energy, psychic and physical, to discipline a child lovingly, to work supportively with a
child on a project, to spend an afternoon relaxing with a child
in the park, to take a child to a museum, to participate in an
event at the child's school, or even to read the child a bedtime
story or to talk seriously with the child at the child's initiative.
That is where the great losses to the family from the bad economic times occur.

According to a recent poll, three-quarters of those responding
believe that parents do not spend enough time with their children and that it is much harder to be a parent today than formerly. Half believe that parents shirk their responsibilities. [11]
When questioned separately, about half of both teachers and
parents report that most or many parents leave their children
on their own too much after school, fail to discipline their children, fail to motivate their children so that they want to learn
in school, take too little interest in their children's education,
and neglect to see that their children's homework gets done. [12]
Regardless of whether the poll data reflect reality or not, most
adults recognize that it is much easier to provide fast foods, to
turn on the television, to encourage the teenager to take a job
after school, or even to leave the household than it is to engage
in the individually unnecessary but cumulatively essential activities that provide genuine nurturing for a child.

Affluent families have also come to realize that the rearing
of a child is not something that can be purchased either through

psychiatrists' fees or fashionable Reeboks. Rather, childrearing must be provided by adults, either family members or others, who have the commitment, energy, and resources. Today more families have the commitment than either the energy or the resources, but commitment alone without the others will not provide the members of the next generation with the support they need. Good intentions without good deeds are not enough.

Personal Fulfillment

While anti-intellectualism and a shortage of money inhibit the ability of many American families to be supportive of their children's educations, they are not the only explanation for the difficulties. Within the last generation the search for personal fulfillment that previously embraced many elements of family life has turned singular. Too many adults, including parents, seek happiness primarily through activities that bring pleasure to themselves, not through developing activities and relationships with others. A characteristic new magazine of the 1980s was called *Self*. Robert Bellah and his colleagues, in a book entitled *Habits of the Heart*, describe the middle-class American individualist sensibility as devoid of traditional religious or ethical expression or of community responsibility.[13]

Attaining what pleases oneself, preferably immediately, is more desirable than attaining something that would be satisfying in the long term. Increased use of drugs and alcohol and sexual promiscuity both meet the standard of instant gratification. That which is difficult or unpleasant is to be avoided. A stark example of this behavior is that of a father who leaves his wife and children and fails to provide support, either financial or emotional, while pursuing what he considers a more fulfilling life-style less burdened by familial obligations. Another, less stark but widespread example of this attitude is the young woman in Columbus, Ohio, who was asked by a reporter if she read newspapers. She replied, "Sort of," explaining that she skipped the front page: "There's more bad news on the front page. I like to go to the local news; it's the fun news."[14]

Families have their share of fun news, but they also contain hard work and bad news. Most of all, families require long-term sustenance and do not provide simple, immediate pleasures only. While there are immense joys in family life in both the short and the long term, there are also many moments of drudgery, concern, frustration, disappointment, and annoyance. These do not fit well in a culture that extols the virtues of youth, money, fashion, expensive consumption, and immediate gratification. The popularity of Jane Fonda's workout techniques is not provided by the single working mother after an eight-hour workday, a one-hour commute, supper with her two children, and some supervised study and bedtime reading followed by baths and bed for all three. She has no time for aerobics, and those who do typically are not deep in the throes of sustaining a family under the difficult conditions that the 1990s present. Both the culture and the economy of the United States currently are much more supportive of Americans who try to improve themselves than of those who try to improve the lives of their children.

Communities

Three factors, then, inhibit the ability of adults to provide the educational foundation that children need: ambivalence about academic achievement, poverty, and excessive concern with the self. The communities in which the adults and children live often reinforce these conditions.

The community of Odessa, Texas, powerfully illustrates sentiments toward education that diminish learning and extol athletics, particularly football. Recently portrayed by H. G. Bissinger in *Friday Night Lights: A Town, a Team, and a Dream*, Odessa's adults seem to orient their autumns, if not their lives, around the fortunes of the high school football team. The academic learning of the players is not taken seriously, only their

athletic performance. Even the health of the players is sometimes sacrificed to the adult townspeople's obsession with
winning.[15]

In another kind of community example, many poor families
in America are forced to live in neighborhoods so lacking in
services that energy that might productively be spent on children
must be expended on keeping the family in food. Until the recent
arrival of a Pathmark supermarket, residents of the central ward
of Newark, New Jersey, had to travel several miles by bus to
shop for groceries. The process of simply getting milk, bread,
and detergent while balancing a baby in one arm and a toddler
in the other and clambering on and off the buses to and from
the distant store was exhausting. Exhausted adults are likely to
rely on less demanding ways of engaging their children, such as
turning on the television, rather than on more active and beneficial modes, such as doing a puzzle with the toddler, building a model with the ten-year-old, or supervising a reluctant
thirteen-year-old's homework. Most of us take the path of least
resistance when we are tired, and while that is understandable,
it may not be beneficial for the children in our care. When
communities make daily living difficult, everybody suffers.

A third community example is suburban Los Angeles, where
commuting times are long, job turnover is frequent, geographic
mobility is great, condominiums are common, religious institutions are weak, community volunteer organizations are few,
health clubs are ubiquitous, and divorce rates are high. Here,
too often, children do not fit smoothly into an adult life-style
that focuses on individual enhancement and that has few community supports for either parents or children. When social life
is centered at the Nautilus machine or in the bar, rather than
at the backyard picnic or the Scouts' potluck supper, a parent
may find nurturing a child difficult. In such neighborhoods the
responsibilities for childrearing, which in other communities
involve a large and diverse group of family, friends, and neighbors, devolve onto a very small number of persons: one or two
parents, the part-time sitter, the child's teacher. Regardless of

how committed this tiny group is, the child needs and deserves
more sustained adult attention and involvement than that.

Worlds Apart

Thus, families, which are the most formative influence in children's lives, are frequently not as supportive of children's education as they need to be. While that may not have been a
problem in the past, when expectations for education were
lower, it is a problem now. National expectations for children's
education, expressed in the many reports on education of the
last decade, are exceeding parental expectations now, and neither parents nor the schools have caught up with the new
demand that more children learn more. Further, the local community in which the family lives is likely to reinforce the family's
values. The problem becomes exacerbated when families do not
feel connected with the one institution whose primary mission
is education, the school, and in many communities that connection is weak. As Sara Lawrence Lightfoot has written, families
and schools are often "worlds apart." There is no dearth of literature on the topic; there is, however, a shortage of mechanisms
by which to bridge these two worlds. [16]

For years school people have blamed parents for sending
their children to school unprepared for learning. As a Greenwich
Village principal observed nearly seventy-five years ago, "People
behave as if there were no other agency in the community than
the school through which anything could be done. Do you know,
I think if it were possible, the parents would be glad to have
the teachers have maternity leave so that they would have their
children for them!" More recently, the principal of South Boston
High School entreated his dubious faculty to recognize that the
parents send the schools the best children they have. But when
a group of regional winners of the Teacher of the Year awards
were recently asked what was the biggest problem they faced,
51 percent replied "parental apathy." [17]

Families, too, often feel unwelcome in a cooperative relationship with the schools, because the schools continue to organize themselves in ways that are antithetical to family routines. Meetings are scheduled at times when parents are working. The daily school schedule continues to assume that there is a caregiver waiting at home for each youngster in early afternoon. The annual calendar is based on the assumption that some responsible person is always available to look after children during the three-month summer vacation, the two-week Christmas vacation, and the one-week spring vacation, not to mention the occasional school holiday. Today few parents find these school arrangements convenient or conducive to cooperation.

Family or community members with special skills or experiences that might be both valuable and interesting supplements to the curriculum often do not feel encouraged to participate in the school program. Somehow, they believe, the teachers can never find an opportunity to fit them into the school day. School inflexibility keeps them from contributing. As higher proportions of the U.S. population have college degrees, the teachers and administrators no longer have the exclusive educational expertise that characterized them in the early years of this century when they were among the most highly educated persons in the town. Both in the places where they do have more education than the other residents and in those where they do not, school people have been criticized for failing to encourage lay participation in the schools. Many schools traditionally have had strong Booster Clubs, composed typically of parents and local folks who take pride in their athletic programs; they have had nothing comparable for their academic activities, which should be the heart of the schools' endeavors.

Change is necessary. It is unlikely to come, however, unless families take the initiative to make children's education a priority. Some families already have committed great effort and energy to their children's educations; others have not, preferring to take the easier route of letting the child decide whether to study or not. Many youngsters find other activities more compelling. Politicians wisely understand that legislation will not bring fundamental improvement for children unless there is support within the families themselves. Political action requires pressure, and unless those most directly affected by a proposed change push for it, there is little likelihood that it will occur. This is particularly true of legislation affecting childrearing, in view of our longstanding reluctance to let the long arm of the law reach into private relationships. If we are to believe the Teachers of the Year who proclaim parental apathy their most difficult challenge, then some significant fraction of parents will need to change their attitudes and behaviors in order to become more supportive of their children's educations.

Coalitions are always valuable when the goal is to bring about change. Thus, the families with children to be educated may wish to make common cause with others, particularly since those of us without school-age children make up the majority of the population. The contributors to the many reports decrying the educational inadequacies of American youth, the readers of those reports, business leaders who find employees ill-prepared, educators who attempt to teach the young, citizens worried about the future of our country—all these segments of American society share with families concern about the education of young people and the ability of the schools to instruct them adequately. Together we may be able to bring about some changes that will benefit American children, and what benefits American children eventually benefits us all. What might those changes be?

Helping Schools Fit Families

The schedules of schools and families are a bad fit. Schools still expect families to adjust to the schools' routine, and that is very difficult for many families. Schools need to change, because accommodating to the constraints faced by families would be better for children's lives in general and for their educations. The schools should be interested in enhancing both.

As we have seen, given the changes in the American family over the last several decades, a school, which is organized around an agrarian calendar and the assumption that either a mother, a hired girl, or a big sister is waiting at home, does not mesh with the realities of modern urban America. Only about 2 percent of American families still live on working farms where children are needed in the summer for harvests. Only about a quarter of school-age children have a mother who is not employed outside the home. Further, for the quarter of all American children who are poor and the half of American black children who are poor, the varied services available to them are spread all over the community. Rarely are services other than schooling located at the school, the one place all children are all required to go. This is a ridiculous situation.[18]

Rationality and practicality demand adjustment in school schedules. Given the reality of much poor pedagogy in schools today, it would be premature to argue for universal extension of the school year and school day for instructional purposes. It will not make sense to mandate increases in the school day or year until there is good reason to believe that the additional time will be well spent. But it is clear that the school building itself should be utilized more efficiently for the benefit of children. At present most buildings are open to children only about 180 days per year and then often for less than eight hours a day. We do not run train stations or air terminals that way. Why should we limit schools? The school building should be opened early in the morning and not closed until the evening. Before and after classes the building should house various services that need not be provided by school personnel. These might include breakfast and snacks organized by the health department, athletic programs coordinated by volunteers, play groups and naps supervised by daycare providers, tutoring programs, clubs, and special interest organizations sponsored by either the local recreation authority or private entities. In addition, the building could serve as the location of offices of the welfare department, the health department, the social security administration, legal aid, and other publicly or privately funded associations that provide services to children and to families. It might also provide

space for elderly citizens to meet (and to mix a bit with the
children) or for the homeless to be served an early dinner (assisted by junior and senior high school students providing public
service). Obviously not all these activities might go on in each
school, but the principle of using the school building to provide
a greater variety of services to children and to the community
would be beneficial to families.

To the question of why such a reasonable idea has not been
implemented, a common response is that bureaucratic obstacles
prevent such integration of services. Professionals in education
are not trained with professionals in health or social work and
consequently do not have informal networks that would facilitate
their working together. Publicly funded activities—federal,
state, and local—all come with extensive regulatory requirements and reporting rules that make cooperation among agencies
difficult. Furthermore, schools do not want to have to bother
with outside groups using their space. Certainly these obstacles
exist, but for the sake of children and families they must be
overcome through political pressure, inventiveness, commitment, and administrative skill.

One concrete reason why the school building is not open
longer is simply that in many places the school custodian's contract does not permit it without exorbitant overtime pay. In many
communities the custodian does not even report to the school
principal and his (rarely her) salary exceeds that of many teachers. The most common excuse offered by school people for why
their building cannot be open longer hours for the benefit of
children is that they cannot deal with the custodian. Political
muscle should be applied to remedy this situation.

The custodian matter is a metaphor for the bad fit between
schools and families. Its resolution would be tricky, would require some political compromise, but it is not an insoluble problem. Rather, it is an example of how a minor but pesky issue
can stall efforts at fundamental reform if there is not a strong
enough push for the reform itself. Although it is widely recognized that the schools' programs are not meshing with family

life, until recently there has not been much serious effort to provide an all-day, all-year supervised and safe environment at the school building. Families are supposed to cope on their own, to locate the disparate services for which they are eligible. The result is a generation of latchkey children without benefit of services.

Nearly forty years ago an order of Episcopal nuns, the Community of the Holy Spirit, organized a private school on the Upper West Side of Manhattan, St. Hilda's and St. Hugh's. It offered a conventional academic program and for an additional fee provided "play group" for children aged three and up in the early morning and until late afternoon and all day in the summer. Neighbors referred somewhat bemusedly to the school and its nuns as a medieval bastion in the sinful city. Although scholarships were available, it was still an expensive endeavor for families to send their children to the nuns, and the clientele remained mostly middle class, drawing heavily in the early days on the children of Protestant clergy, impoverished academics, and European and Asian immigrants. Academically and socially it never achieved the cachet of Brearley, Trinity, or Collegiate, the schools of choice for the Columbia University faculty in the neighborhood and for many others, but it did provide a safe and supervised environment for children. The school continues, though it has undergone many changes, largely as a result of retirements and departures of the nuns in the order. Incidentally, the nuns were their own custodians.

Across the country there are many scattered examples similar to St. Hilda's and St. Hugh's. Some are also in the public schools, which educate over 88 percent of our children. In San Diego, for example, a comprehensive center on the campus of Hamilton Elementary School gives families access to services offered by the county Department of Social Services; health professionals; city housing, parks and recreation, library, and police services; school district counselors; and the San Diego Community College District. This pilot program, titled New Beginnings, has received financial support from the Stuart and Danforth Foundations, and the program hopes to be a model for future collaboration among public agencies.[19] The problem with such efforts is their isolation and their scarcity. The public schools need to overcome the bureaucratic obstacles preventing them from changing their schedules and from providing broader services. Conceptually the issue is quite easy; politically it is very difficult. That is why coalitions of parents and others must push for it.

Lisbeth B. Schorr, in her book entitled *Within Our Reach*, encourages us to surmount these barriers to providing health, educational, and social services to children. She also summarizes three common elements that characterize such successful programs: (1) they are comprehensive and intensive, requiring active collaboration across professional and bureaucratic boundaries; (2) they deal with the child as part of a family, and with the family as part of a neighborhood or a community; and (3) they have staff with the time, training, and skills necessary to build relationships of trust and respect with children and families.[20]

If the schools are to provide a broader array of activities, such as health programs, child care, and welfare services, then new administrative arrangements are required. While the building must be the site of the services, the educators who work there need not be in overall charge of the variety of programs housed there. The skills to build community support for these varied programs, as Schorr rightly notes, may be different from the skills needed to inspire children to read. Some jobs are appropriate for administrators, others for educators. Perhaps schools could lease space in a building from a community organization for the part of the day devoted to instruction, while the community organization would maintain the building and provide the other services. Both tradition and regulations militate against such a plan at present, but if we want our children healthy, educated, and cared for, then we need some new arrangements.

The Comer Process

Probably the best-known figure today demonstrating how families and schools can work together for the benefit of children is James Comer, a professor of child psychiatry at Yale University. Comer, a native of East Chicago, Indiana, where his mother was a domestic and his father a steelworker, has written about his family's commitment to education (*Maggie's American Dream: The Life and Times of a Black Family*) and about his belief in the importance of schools (*School Power: Implications of an Intervention Project*).[21] In his life and in his profession he has brought together this dual interest in promoting family and schooling and his belief that the two institutions must collaborate, particularly in the case of poor and minority youngsters. Comer has worked on this subject in the New Haven public schools since the War on Poverty days when it was fashionable, through the intervening two decades when such activity was not fashionable. He published *School Power* in 1980 when interest in public schooling for the poor was at its nadir. Comer has persevered to see his ideas and himself the beneficiary of great public attention, accolades, and most recently $15 million from the Rockefeller Foundation to advance his ideas and program.

Comer's fundamental idea is that mutual distrust between educators and many poor and minority families, based on differences in their backgrounds and values, has forced the children to choose either the family values or those of the schools. John Ogbu, a professor of anthropology at the University of California, has made a similar point for black children, arguing that these youngsters face the dilemma of either following their family's survival strategies or abiding by the expectations of the schools and "acting white," thus alienating themselves from their families.[22]

Unlike Ogbu, who is more pessimistic about bridging the gap between black culture and predominantly white and middle-class school values, Comer believes that the gap can be closed if parents or their surrogates are involved more intimately with the schools. The Comer Process, as it is now called, stresses child development as the basis for understanding children's learning and encourages parents to participate in school policymaking through representation on governance and management teams, in activities supporting the school program, and in various events at the school. The intention is for parents and educators to meet and work together in different settings so that each will come to appreciate the other more and the differences between them will diminish. This cooperation will, in turn, build support in the home for the goals and procedures of school.

Comer's approach has the advantage of persistence and practicality, both enormous strengths in educational reform, which too often has been both impulsive and impractical. Initially supported relatively modestly by the National Institute of Mental Health, the Maurice Falk Medical Foundation, the Ford Foundation, and the New Haven Public Schools and Yale University, Comer has now found broad acclaim both because his ideas and implementation are good and because the timing is right. The American public has finally recognized that the issues that concern Comer must concern them too, and the Rockefeller Foundation, with new leadership and a new vice-president in charge of minority youth issues, has significantly reentered the educational fray after a near absence of about a quarter-century. This support is heartening, and it is to be hoped that it may be a harbinger of other initiatives to address these issues of collaboration between families and schools.

Other Collaborations

Thus far, Comer's plan is the most comprehensive for involving families and educators in collaborative efforts for children's education, but there are many other prototypes already in existence around the country that could be developed more fully. For example, athletic booster clubs could be paralleled by academic ones, which would draw professionals in the community into coaching children in their specialties. American children did well in the international Mathematics Olympiad in 1991, but not as

well as the Soviet team, which had had a year of special preparation while the U.S. team had had only six weeks. Informal
Math Olympiad clubs in schools, if they were supported not
just by overworked math teachers but also by mathematically
proficient parents or other adults, could be a big boost to American expertise in mathematics. Similarly, writing clubs geared
to helping youngsters write regularly and proficiently could be
overseen not just by overextended English teachers but by other
adults with a command of standard English prose or poetry,
whose writing might be more varied and thus more interesting
to kids.

The talents of native speakers of languages other than English
are another great underused resource in America. Most cannot
be certified as teachers under existing state requirements. Neither have they been sought to supplement regular classwork by
foreign language departments, which have seen their enroll-
ments plummet just as the proportion of students whose native
language is not English has increased. Some teachers of foreign
languages seem to believe they are in some other line of work
from those who teach non-English-speaking children. Foreign
language instruction in the schools traditionally has been for the
elite, college-bound students, and many instructors have en-
joyed identifying with their students' destinies. Bilingual instruction, in contrast, has been for immigrants, many of whom
are not part of the school elite, and their teachers, too, have
shared their students' status in the school. The gap between the
two groups of teachers has become virtually unbridgeable in
many schools. Finding articulate native speakers of languages
that students speak at home, whether they be parents or not,
and incorporating them into classroom instruction with regular
foreign language teachers or into other school activities, would
be a big improvement in many communities. Too often such
native speakers are simply used as paraprofessionals or aides to
translate and to resolve thorny administrative problems that children and parents have with schools, not treated as instructors
with a skill valued by the entire school.

The interaction between family and school becomes more

complex when students have babies. A promising innovation is
the parenting programs that have been instituted in many
schools, intended chiefly for adolescents who are prematurely
becoming parents. In the 1970s imaginative efforts in Philadelphia, led by Peter Buttenweiser, brought together prenatal care,
child care instruction and service, and parenting classes at the
Durham Child Development Center. Today we are again see-
ing efforts of schools, particularly in cities, to establish special
programs for their young-mother students, more rarely for their
young-father students, and for the babies, their future students.[23] When asked recently what innovation would most improve the high school in Boston with which his company was
paired, a CEO replied, "a nursery and day care for the children
of the high school students so the mothers can remain in school."

Most parenting instruction focuses upon principles of health,
nutrition, and child development for infants and for young parents.[24] This is a vitally important effort, but another needed
focus is upon adults who care for adolescents. As has long been
known, and as David Hamburg has observed in recent Carnegie
Corporation documents, the early years of adolescence are a
particularly difficult time.[25] The adults responsible for adolescents often take the easiest course: letting them go their own
way and ignoring signs of incipient trouble. Here some instruction and support for parenting dilemmas would serve both the
families and the schools. An adolescent who is having trouble at
home is often in difficulty at school, and vice versa. Therefore,
it is in the self-interest of both home and school to work together
to deal with the turmoil of adolescence. Discussions among parents, students, educators, and employers, for example, might
reveal a good deal about the relative importance of work versus
study in high school students' lives. Additional discussions with
employers about the kinds of skills they seek in entry-level employees might also prove illuminating for students, parents, and
educators. Further conversation about opportunities for mobility
within companies might prove useful as well. Many schools currently sponsor Career Days at which some of these kinds of

topics are covered, but typically they involve the student and the recruiter but neither the parent nor the teacher, both of whom would benefit from the substance of the meeting and from the opportunity to get together to consider options for the student. Companies might explain, for example, why they find students with algebra more suitable employees than those with business arithmetic and what the long-term possibilities are for each in their companies.

Not only companies but also colleges could profitably engage in discussions with high school students, their teachers, and their parents. Like the companies, colleges generally meet only with the student or occasionally with the guidance counselor. Broader groups should be involved, and the college recruiter should be able to discuss more than just the quality of the dormitories and the cost of tuition. Rather, the college emissaries ought to be able to speak knowledgeably about the academic workload on their campuses and the kind of academic preparation faculty members expect in their undergraduates. Parents, teachers, and students need to participate in these kinds of discussions together.

One of the most common problems troubling adolescents and their parents is school-related social life. What are the ground rules about chaperons, appropriate dress, drinking, where parties are held, and what time parties should end? Some of the best examples of resolving this issue are the initiatives taken by local schools surrounding that penultimate high school event, the prom. Staggered by the spectacle of prom nights of wild excess and expense with rented evening clothes, limousines, and all-night parties lubricated with alcohol, a number of communities have organized prom events that eliminate such displays. For a community—students, parents, school people, and other adults—to agree about prom rules enhances the likelihood that community norms may also be established for less symbolically significant social events.

Children and Communities

Not all of children's social life revolves around school activities, of course. Much is based in the community where the family lives. The community's values regarding appropriate behavior and activities for young people are vital as children seek to find their places in the world outside their homes. If the community reinforces the family's values, then those values are likely to have deeper meaning for the youngster: whereas if the family's and the community's values are at variance, the youngster's confusion is likely to increase.

Back in what so many people now think was the Golden Age, one of the principal ways youngsters became acquainted with the community outside of school was in youth groups. For boys, and more recently for girls too, there were athletic programs such as Little League. For rural Americans there was 4-H; for urban Americans there were Girls' or Boys' Clubs and one of the Y's: YMCA, YWCA, YMHA, or YWHA. Small-town America specialized in Scouts. Across America religious institutions organized groups for their young people, from Vacation Bible School to Methodist Youth Fellowship to Canterbury Club to Catholic Youth Organization to Federation of Temple Youth. With the increase in women's employment outside the home during the last several decades these organizations, staffed heavily by volunteers, have fallen on hard times. In addition, many of the religious groups have turned their attention away from youth toward social issues such as homelessness or AIDS.

While there is no doubt that employment patterns, particularly of women, who have carried the brunt of nonprestigious volunteer work, have limited participation in community organizations, there remains a growing and as yet insufficiently tapped resource that could provide volunteer service, namely the retirees, who are retiring earlier and living longer. Many middle managers who now retire somewhat abruptly and precipitously in their mid-fifties have been so busy climbing the corporate ladder that they have had little experience in volunteer work or in community organizations. Yet they have many years ahead of them in which their talents could be used to help young people. Traditionally, adult leadership of local youth organizations, such as the Scouts, has come from parents of the children involved. But these are the people, as we have seen, who are so stretched by demands on their time and energy that they may not be able to assume these roles. Retirees could undertake these tasks with great benefit to the youngsters, to themselves, and to the parents who cannot shoulder these added responsibilities.

Mentoring, a concept currently enjoying a renewed vogue of popularity, comes in a variety of forms. We used to call it simply friendship between an adult and a child. Today it may mean a one-to-one relationship between an academic tutor and a tutee, or it may mean a personal relationship between an adult and a child without specific academic focus. It may also take the form of leadership of a youth organization. There are many other varieties, but each allows children to get to know adults other than parents and teachers, as in an earlier time they would have informally through the neighborhood, religious organizations, ethnic social clubs, or extended family. These contacts are extraordinarily valuable for the children, introducing them to sympathetic grownups who can help them steer their little boat into the world. The relationships are also very beneficial to the adults, who provide genuine community service by helping others and thereby also provide additional meaning for their own lives. For overextended parents, these additional adults caring for their children are a godsend, and parents should seek such support in their communities.[26]

Employment: Too Much, Too Little

When children reach adolescence, youth organizations face strong competition from employment. Given a choice between collecting the badges to become an Eagle Scout and bagging groceries in the local supermarket, adolescents seem to prefer the latter. Although, as noted in Chapter 1, sociologists and educators in the 1960s and 1970s considered part-time work beneficial to youngsters, in the 1990s many have come to regard it as excessive. Some parents appear less convinced.

No one would seriously challenge the benefit of five or ten hours of paid employment per week during the school year. At the minimum wage, that would produce about $40, probably not enough to make a car payment but enough to buy a nice shirt or, after two weeks, some middle-of-the-line running shoes. A generation ago during the school year boys delivered newspapers, cut lawns, pumped gas, and worked in grocery stores while girls primarily baby-sat. Rarely did these activities add up to ten hours a week. With the funds saved, one might buy a bicycle, but it was not unusual to save the money for some later use, such as college, or to contribute it to the family economy. In the summer the work options increased. My own first summer job was detasseling corn and pollinating tomatoes on farms near my Indiana home.

Today the situation is quite different. A high school guidance counselor in Elgin, Illinois, recently reported that nearly all the juniors and seniors and a growing number of freshmen and sophomores at her 2,800-student high school have part-time jobs. "It's a black hole," she said. Teachers now allocate class time for students to finish homework assignments they cannot do after school because they work. The result is a lowering of standards and a "dumbing down" of the curriculum for all the students, those who work and those who do not. "Give students a paycheck with their own name on it, and they lose sight of everything else. They love that instant gratification. The rewards for good grades are vague, abstract and distant. But with that paycheck they can get the clothes, the cars and the stereo equipment that everyone else has," the counselor concluded.[27]

A survey in New Hampshire revealed that 70 percent of all teenagers are now holding jobs and that more than 84 percent of those in grades ten through twelve are working, with 45 percent of them putting in more than 20 hours per week.[28] Not surprisingly, these students are not doing well in school.

Generally these youngsters report that they take easier courses and do not do much homework because they simply do not have the time or the energy. One New Hampshire seventeen-year-old, whose father says he does not need the money and can do with it what he likes, works about thirty hours a week at a fast-food restaurant in order to pay for his $6,100 Escort GT and his $5,600 Kawasaki motorcycle, about which he admits, "It's kind of a frivolous thing." Although he had a "not good" junior year academically, he is working to improve in his senior year and has received only one C, but this is at the price of lost sleep, which averages only six hours per night.[29] For this youngster, the values of consumerism have overwhelmed the values of learning. Families who permit their children to engage in this amount of employment during the school year are fostering a penchant for the acquisition of material goods and for debt while damaging both the children's opportunities for the future and their health. There is no excuse for it.

Community incentives to reduce or eliminate this kind of employment in the short term are nil. Tired teenagers like the fast-food employee are less likely to cause a ruckus in the town, and they certainly stimulate the economy with their purchases. Employers can hire these kids at low wages and on a part-time basis, thus often avoiding having to provide the benefits and job security that adults would seek. But youngsters who grow up in these ways without strong academic backgrounds become the adult workers about whom American business complains and for whom business provides remedial instruction. Fast-food establishments may not do much of that, but IBM and Motorola do, and in the long run communities need the latter kinds of businesses in their towns more than they need the former.

A broader study of national patterns of employment and achievement of high school students, analyzing the data from the National Assessment of Educational Progress (NAEP), reveals patterns consistent with the evidence from Illinois and New Hampshire. Scores in mathematics, science, history, literature, and reading all decline with more than fifteen hours of work per

week. Among eleventh-graders nationally boys are more likely
to work than girls, and whites more likely than blacks. Perhaps
the most startling conclusion is that students working the higher
number of hours are more likely to come from families in which
both parents work full time.[30] Here again we see the trend
exemplified by the New Hampshire youngster and his father;
the kids are working for money to buy things they and their
families do not need, and in doing so they are sacrificing their
academic achievement. This is the late-twentieth-century version of American anti-intellectualism and its demeaning of the
value of learning.

Serious as the problem of too much working is, the problem
of no jobs for black youth, especially young men, is worse. Between 1964 and 1986 the fraction of black male students ages
sixteen and seventeen who were working declined from 26 percent to 11 percent. In the same period employment for young
white male students rose from 30 percent to 36 percent and
that for young black female students from 11 percent to 17
percent.[31] Undoubtedly these figures reflect the social chaos of
the urban neighborhoods in which many of these black males
live and the greater impact of that chaos on them than upon
their sisters.

The lack of family and community support for these young
black men and the danger in which they find themselves has
led some communities to create special programs for them.
Both New York City and Milwaukee, for example, have been
considering the establishment of special schools limited to black
males, where their academic prowess, self-esteem, and workplace skills could be enhanced in a supportive environment that
would include many successful black men as teachers and role-
models. Whether schools limited to black males are either desirable or constitutional is questionable, but there is no doubt
that adolescent black males in the cities need enormous help in
making the transition to productive and personally fulfilling adult
lives. If their low rates of adolescent employment were matched
by high levels of academic achievement, then one would not

worry so about them, but they do not rank high on either. Clearly both issues—achievement and employment—need to be addressed.

Adolescent employment is a complicated issue. No one can quarrel with the value of limited (ten hours per week or less) paid work during the school year or full-time work during the summer vacation. The danger for many youngsters is too much work during the school year, which, among other disadvantages, leads to reduced academic achievement. For others, the problem is too little work. Either too much or too little work may make it more difficult for a young person to complete a smooth transition from schooling to employment. Working too much may both limit development of academic skills and encourage youngsters to emphasize the acquisition of consumer goods. The combination leaves such young people in low-level jobs, unable to establish themselves as economically independent or to secure promotions to more demanding and secure employment. Working too little, on the other hand, may prevent one from learning the skills necessary in the workplace. Without those and with experience in a neighborhood where many are unemployed and discouraged, many are unable to find a job at all. The unemployment rate of black teenagers in 1988 was 32 percent, more than six times the national average.[32]

From the point of view of subsequent employment, by far the best strategy is to go to college and complete a demanding major. For those who cannot or do not choose college, the transition to permanent, economically stable employment in America is difficult, and heavy part-time employment during high school with the likely consequence of lowered academic learning is likely to make it even more difficult. Harder still is the transition for those with poor academic records and no successful work experience. We lack in the United States effective means of smoothing the transition from school to work that other nations have achieved, particularly Germany with its apprenticeship systems that are closely tied to and developed by its industries. Families and communities need to recognize that most employ-

ers value both academic achievement and the capacity to solve
new problems. They also want employees who understand the
explicit and implicit rules of the workplace. Some employment
in adolescence is valuable, but either too much or too little is
damaging. Families, as well as communities and business, have
an obligation to understand this and to prevent adolescents from
undertaking too much employment while assisting them in finding some work experience.[33]

Families are their children's first educators. The communities
in which they live are the second. Both these experiences pre-
cede and cumulatively exceed the influence of schooling. If the
family and the community strongly support education, then the
likelihood that a child will succeed in school and in life is profoundly increased. If they do not, then success is more elusive.
State legislatures cannot demand that families limit their television watching as they can regulate the activities of schools.
Nor is the federal government likely to prohibit teenagers from
working thirty hours a week during the school year. But the
families and the communities in which they reside can become
much more sensitive to the effect of these practices upon their
children.

The late-twentieth-century analogue of my Danish grandfather's skepticism about learning is the New Hampshire father
whose seventeen-year-old son is working at a fast-food restaurant. Both fathers believed in hard work for their sons, and
neither apparently saw extended education as important. Both
reflect the pervasive anti-intellectualism that has hindered this
country's commitment to broad academic learning for its people.
The contemporary version also has a profound desire for material
objects. The respect for their sons' hard work that both fathers
share is valuable for the country, but the accompanying anti-
intellectualism and materialism are not. A family that endorses
the seventeen-year-old's long hours so that he can buy a new
car and a new motorcycle while his grades slide is supporting a
set of values that are antithetical to both the youngster's and the

nation's healthy development. The boy needs to reduce his hours at work, if necessary getting rid of either his car or his motorcycle or both, so that he can sleep more and learn more. His family should insist upon it. That would be better for him and for all of us.

· 3 ·

Government

When Richard Riley became governor of South Carolina in 1979, he launched his administration with a realistic and persuasive summons: "We in South Carolina can't become first in public schools in the next four years, but we can become first in first grade." To a remarkable degree South Carolina under Riley's leadership succeeded in rallying public opinion to raise the educational expectations of children and families and in mobilizing will and resources to provide universal kindergarten (a new notion in the state) and mandatory programs for four-year-olds deemed "at risk." "First in first grade" may be hard to measure, but it is not hard to grasp. South Carolinians took hold, and their little children are better off than they used to be.

Riley believed in convincing the citizens of the state that all of them must support better education for children. The leadership for such an effort, he opined, must come not just from governors, or those who write to the *New York Times*, but also from black grandmothers and others who are leaders in their churches and hence in their communities. Together they improved South Carolina's public education.

Riley's efforts in South Carolina exemplified governmental educational reform in the 1980s. During the past decade the major actors in school reform have been state governments, which now provide about 50 percent of the funding for public schools. Governors, many of them in southern states that traditionally have had both weak public school systems and weak economies, have pushed for better schools. Their efforts have ranged from Lamar Alexander's plan in Tennessee to use merit pay for teachers as a stimulus to improvement to Bill Clinton's determination in Arkansas to expand programs for young children. Even Mississippi, which has frequently trailed the states in school achievement, under the governorship of William Winter took major steps during the decade to improve the health of children and to recruit outstanding teachers. In 1990 Kentucky's legislature passed comprehensive legislation that established a new system of funding to help close the gap between the richest and poorest school districts in the state, and that mandated new criteria for assessing outcomes to be achieved by children and schools based on such factors as student health, dropout rates, and attendance.[1]

Most of these initiatives seemed to be motivated by state government's recognition both that the young needed a stronger education in order to prosper as adults in the twenty-first century and that the states needed a more capable workforce in order to attract industry to bolster their economies. These two goals came together in the minds of state leaders, and the result was much talk and some action on behalf of children and schools.

In New England, however, where many of the schools were highly regarded for much of this century and where the economy flourished during the 1980s, educational reform efforts have been much more sluggish. As the 1990s bring economic hard times and reduced state revenues to that region, the outlook for educational reform is not promising unless state leaders can mobilize their constituencies to invest in the young. Thus far they have not been able to do so. Herman B. Leonard compared the choices made by Massachusetts in its public spending to choices made by other states and found that, after controlling for circumstances and costs, spending on elementary and sec-

ondary education in Massachusetts fell during the 1980s and in
1988 was about 10 percent less than what other states were
spending on education. This decrease occurred despite the fact
that the state now has significant numbers of immigrant children
whose native language is not English and for whom American
schools are more difficult than they were for the Yankee youngsters of the past.[2]

In the nation as a whole, state spending on education did
not increase dramatically during the 1980s. Between 1979 and
1989 overall state spending rose from $7.28 per $100 of personal
income to $7.80, but state spending for elementary and secon-
dary education actually decreased by one penny. Support for
public higher education during the same period experienced a
similar decline of three cents. Furthermore, during the decade
the federal share of elementary and secondary expenses dropped
considerably. The major increases in state spending were for
prisons, Medicaid, and health and hospitals. The major loser
was welfare. This is hardly a pattern of expenditures likely to
help the young.[3]

Typically states and communities have reacted to criticisms
of their schools not by increasing resources but by mandating
more tests, tests that examine the students but grade the schools.
Schools are thought to be "good" if the children score well on
tests, and schools are thought to be "bad" if the children score
poorly on tests. Teachers' salaries often follow these general
trends. In Massachusetts, for example, among the highest salary
schedules in the state are those in the most affluent Boston
suburbs, where family and community mores reinforce student
learning. Conversely, salaries are lowest where learning is most
difficult. Affluent, suburban Newton, with a per capita income
of $22,918, pays its teachers an average salary of $44,308, but
financially strapped Chelsea, with per capita income at $9,728,
pays its teachers only $26,089.[4]

In the enthusiasm for extended assessment programs, which
allegedly make the schools accountable for their students' performances, relatively little attention is given to the fit between

the material that children are expected to know and what is actually taught in the classroom. For example, children who grow up in households that prize accurate and effective use of English are likely to do well on tests of reading and grammar, largely as a consequence of their home background, not as a result of their classroom English instruction. I remember sitting as a little girl at the Morton School in West Lafayette, Indiana, taking one of my first standardized tests and answering the questions about correct usage and grammar. As I pondered whether it was correct to write "between you and I" or "between you and me," I remembered only my mother's repeated corrections of my speech, never any formal instruction on this subject from Miss Boyd, Miss Daniels, Miss Kent, or Mr. Davis, my elementary school teachers. Yet under the present arrangements those schools and teachers whose children score high in English are praised and rewarded for good results for which they are only partially responsible. Meanwhile, those children for whom school has been the dominant academic force in their life are likely to do less well on the tests, and their schools and teachers will be criticized accordingly, although, in fact, the school may have been relatively a much larger contributor to the child's knowledge of academic material than in the case of the children whose parents have instructional propensities.

While it is important and desirable for states and localities to hold their school systems accountable for their students' academic performance, most efforts thus far at such measures of "accountability" are crude and do not truly assess how good a job the schools, as opposed to the families, communities, and society, are doing with their students. They are much better at telling us what a student knows than at determining where the student learned it. Even efforts to tell us what the students know are limited by the kinds of assessments now available, still mostly tests that can be scored by machines. The questions on those instruments may not be the most important indicators of a youngster's knowledge. For example, we do not yet have a paper-and-pencil measure of perseverance or cooperativeness, both essential to complex problem-solving. Thus, pinning our hopes for educational improvement heavily upon measures of assessment and accountability, while fashionable at the moment, is not likely to bring us the results we seek. A much broader strategy for enhancing the education of children is required. While some states are beginning to recognize this need, it is the federal government that has the obligation, ability, and self-interest to foster the human resources of the nation.

The rhetoric of American education is filled with paeans to the virtues of local control of schools. There are many ways in which a country as large and diverse as the United States benefits from a decentralization of its educational system. Nonetheless, if we look at the problems that beset the country as a whole— the problems I have labeled poverty, productivity, participation, and passivity—and if we expect some resolution of them from the schools, then significant action by the federal government is required. The absence of educational leadership from Washington, especially during the 1980s, has intensified many of the problems faced by the schools. There is plenty of room for state and local initiative in educational reform, but the fundamental problems of poverty, single-parent families, inadequate child care, and hopelessness that affect many of our children are in the domain of the country as a whole, not of a beleaguered town with an inadequate tax base. Since the problems are inherently national in scope, federal actions are in order.

For much of our history we in the United States have believed that our strength resulted in important ways from our abundant natural resources, which we tended to define as our minerals, our forests, our fine agricultural lands, and our temperate climate. But over the years we have learned that we cannot live on iron ore and plentiful corn alone; we need people whose minds and motivations fit the challenges of the nation's purposes and problems.

Stimulated in part by international competition, we are re-examining our beliefs about natural resources. Resource-poor Japan has taught us in this generation, as England did in the nineteenth century, that the ability of a nation to mobilize its people's skills, values, and attitudes around national priorities can compensate for a shortage of oil or wheat or hydroelectric power. In the United States we achieved universal elementary education early, and we extended higher education broadly and attained high levels of research. In the United States everyone now reads at a basic level of recognizing "stop" or "go," and we lead the world in attracting scholars to undertake the highest levels of research. Between grade three and Ph.D. level work, however, our record is more mixed. While we extended formal schooling to mass populations earlier than most other countries, we did not expect or enforce high academic standards for all the new students. Consequently, we have a system of broad access in which some students, for reasons of personal motivation, natural aptitude, or family and community pressures, can do very well. Similarly, some students without motivation, aptitude, or pressures can coast from elementary school even into graduate school with few obstacles and little learning. They can also drop out of the formal schooling system, and until recently could usually find work and live reasonably comfortably. The American policy of broad access has enormous educational virtues in its ability either to maintain youngsters in school through a difficult period or to allow them reentry when they become ready for extended education. But with broad access we also need in our schools and colleges more rigorous expectations of academic achievement for everybody. Fulfilling those expectations involves hard work, a notion too often unfamiliar to students.

Americans as a people are very familiar with hard work and with its great supplement, what we have called "Yankee ingenuity." We believe that we built the country on hard work and ingenuity, an honorable and effective combination. These historical cultural icons have not penetrated the world of schooling, however, and they must. The needs of the future require a different kind of hard work, not the physical demands of clearing the stumps from the back forty acres but the demands of psychic discipline of accuracy, efficiency, and economy. Similarly, the ingenuity that is needed is not that of the lonely inventor working in his garage or the isolated farmer repairing his machinery but rather the social ingenuity to work in groups to accomplish more collectively than any one could individually. Finding the motivational strategies to keep people interested in and committed to the task involves new sets of organizational skills.

These new requirements that individuals be able to work together also require higher levels of skill among the individuals themselves. Our citizens today need a broader and deeper core of common knowledge than they did in years past in order to be able to learn new tasks, including new adaptations of technology. When one's job was limited to a finite set of activities and one's ingenuity needed to be applied to a discrete set of problems, then demands for wide-ranging knowledge were limited. Today, however, the jobs are likely to change and the problems to vary, and one is expected to participate collegially with others in mastering new jobs and solving new problems. The change, the variance, and the collegial activity all necessitate changes in the substance and style of learning.

As one manufacturer in upstate New York explained, the entry-level employees in his plant's stockroom now need to be able to computer-code all products and make revisions in the codes according to various manufacturing and distribution specifications. When he began at the plant thirty years ago, entry-level stockroom employees simply loaded boxes onto trucks. The necessary skills have changed dramatically. So too for the managers. In a previous generation a young man could attend an Ivy League college, marry in the Episcopal church, go off to a brokerage firm, join the country club, work and socialize with persons of similar background. Today such a young man finds the competition much stiffer. He will encounter difficulties being admitted to his father's college unless he has done very well in high school. Marriage and family life will likely require more accommodation to his wife's interests than was true in his parents' generation. Jobs are no longer secure, and good entry-level management jobs are no longer limited to Ivy League white

male Episcopalians. His work life and his social life will require
him to cooperate with others quite different from himself. For
this cooperation to work, he and the others will need common
understandings both of academic materials and of cultural traditions. In short, this hypothetical young man faces much higher
demands for knowledge of various kinds than his father did.

As a nation we have believed in supporting our resources
and our industries. We have subsidized soybeans and dairy
farms, not to mention Chrysler. Now we must reconceive our
efforts to invest in the cultivation of our most precious natural
resource, our people. The development of our human resources
begins with their health and continues with their education. We
have made this investment reasonably well in the past with white
males, who have always been a minority in the population but
who have dominated the workforce. In the future white males
will become a minority in the workforce, which will be predominantly made up of women and persons of color. Historically we
have not done well as a nation in educating either of these groups
or, particularly for persons of color, in keeping them healthy.
The old formulas for education, which are dependent on healthy
and well-motivated students, are not working well in the present and will not work in the future. New formulas must be found,
and it is profoundly in the nation's self-interest to identify and
implement them promptly.

National priorities of this magnitude and this degree of urgency fall into the domain of the federal government. It must,
of course, seek support from other sectors in accomplishing this
enormous task. But just as the state of Michigan does not assume
total responsibility for Chrysler or dairy farmers themselves for
milk price supports, so the federal government has a leading
role to play in providing for the health and in enhancing the
educations of Americans. State and local governments will continue to operate the schools, and families will remain the vital
unit for support of children, while institutions of higher education and businesses will have important ancillary roles to play
in improving education. For an issue as vital to the nation as a

whole as education, the federal government must give rhetorical, policy, and fiscal leadership. In recent years its efforts have been largely rhetorical.

The federal government's support for education lies in three principal domains: ensuring children's health, assisting education outside the schools, and aiding school reform. The president's bully pulpit is a useful tool to further each of these efforts. But just as we have considered it important to talk about the need for a strong defense establishment, we have also believed it essential to appropriate funds to be sure that the need was met. The same relationship between rhetoric and funding applies in education, but here the level of funding that has been provided has raised expectations but has utterly failed to meet the needs.

Ensuring Children's Health

Many children grow up just fine without any noticeable help from the government. But many of those without apparent federal aid do benefit indirectly from homes financed with Veteran's Administration mortgages or the savings and loan bailout, from suburbs whose roads and mass transit were developed with federal funds, from parents who were educated either at public universities or at institutions with large federal research awards. A very large portion of our annual state and national expenditures goes to buttressing the capacity of American middle-class families to offer themselves and their children normal and decent lives. Children from such families often do well in school not only because their families and communities want and expect them to do so but also because their families and communities provide plenty of examples of others similarly situated who have done well. These examples provide an important ingredient of motivation. Rare is the child who aspires to and attains success alone. Most children come to believe in themselves because the people around them believe in them and because they are surrounded by examples of others in the community who have prospered.

Not all children are so fortunate. More than half the children in America today will spend some part of their childhood in a single-parent family. As noted earlier, nearly 25 percent of all young American children, and almost half of young black children, live in poverty. Even an only child born into a two-parent family in which one adult works full time at the minimum wage will live at 11 percent below the poverty line. The numbers of children in poverty declined during the 1960s, a consequence both of the economic prosperity of that decade and of the federal legislation of the War on Poverty. Some increase in the numbers in poverty occurred during the 1970s, but the major increases (more than one million more poor children annually) came in the early 1980s.[5] A Fordham University study has revealed that 1987 "was the worst year for children in two decades."[6] As Marian Wright Edelman has observed, "In 1987 the median income of the nation's 1.3 million young black families fell below the amount of money needed to keep a family of four out of poverty. Twenty years ago, the median income of young black families was nearly one and one-half times that poverty level."[7]

The story of the 1980s is that the rich have gotten richer and the poor poorer—and the effects on poor children have been devastating. Largely as a consequence of governmental policies and changes in the economy, poverty has increased dramatically among those who were already on the financial edge, while the affluent have prospered. Consider these figures from the House of Representatives Select Committee on Children, Youth, and Families: average family income among low-income families with children declined by 14 percent between 1979 and 1987, while the income of the highest-income families increased by 19 percent. The poverty rate for American families has increased by 40 percent since 1970. For children living in female-headed households the drop in family income since 1970 is even worse: from $12,136 to $9,838 in 1987 dollars. In 1987 two-thirds of children under age six in female-headed households were living below the poverty line.[8]

Poor children are less likely than their more affluent compatriots to be healthy, and their development is more likely to be rocky, particularly in terms of the mysterious but essential qualities of self-esteem and motivation. Our social welfare legislation today emphasizes treating problems after they have occurred, rather than preventing them. We learned long ago from the field of medicine that prevention is vastly cheaper and easier than treatment after infection, and that remains true whether the disease is viral or social. Up to now our national social and political will have not been strong enough to generate adequate support for such prevention. We know we should engage in prevention, but we have not organized ourselves to do so. In 1988, 20 percent of all American children had no health insurance coverage, up from 17 percent in 1982, and the absence of health insurance is a profound disincentive for seeking anything other than emergency medical care. A dollar spent on children's immunization and metabolic screening saves $14 later, but more than 20 percent of children and more than 50 percent of black children are not fully immunized. Further, the proportion who are not fully immunized is increasing; for example, in 1970, 78 percent of young children were immunized against polio, but in 1985, only 55 percent were. Similarly, the WIC program (Special Supplemental Food Program for Women, Infants, and Children), which provides nutritional information and food supplements for low-income pregnant women and for "nutritionally at risk" children up to age five, addresses a vital need, but it is funded to serve only half of the eligible recipients. A Ford Foundation study published in 1989, *The Common Good*, recommends full funding of both WIC and Head Start and changes in Medicaid to provide health insurance for needy pregnant women and children not covered at present. The estimated additional cost would be $1.7 billion for WIC, $2 billion for Head Start, and $1 billion for Medicaid. Testimony from five CEOs echoed the Ford Foundation report's call for increased funding of WIC. As James Renier of Honeywell put it, "The return on the investment will be worth it—and not too far down the road. Children in this country—and therefore the country itself—face a terrible crisis."[9]

The consequences of this neglect of poor children and the adverse effects upon their health are revealed in a recent international study of social, economic, and health indicators of children in the United States and other developed nations (Australia, Britain, Canada, France, Hungary, Italy, Japan, Norway, the Soviet Union, Sweden, and West Germany). U.S. children are more likely to be poor, to be in a single-parent family, and to be killed before they reach the age of twenty-five than children in any of the other countries. Only the Soviet Union has a higher rate of infant mortality than the United States. In other developed countries, 99 percent of poor families with children receive government assistance; in the United States, only 73 percent do.[10] These figures show the United States at even worse advantage than do the international studies of educational achievement, thereby illustrating the extraordinary efforts of families and schools to overcome the desperate circumstances in which too many American children find themselves.

The Perry Preschool Project, which involved poor, black three- and four-year-olds, provides a clear example of the beneficial effects of preventive action for social development. In Ypsilanti, Michigan, 123 children were randomly placed into either an experimental group that attended a high-quality preschool program or a control group that attended no preschool program. Careful assessments of these children were made through age nineteen. At age nineteen those children who had attended preschool were more likely to have graduated from high school, to be enrolled in an institution of higher education, and to be gainfully employed. Furthermore, those who had attended preschool were less likely to have been placed in special education classes, to have been arrested for committing a crime, to have borne a child, or to have received welfare assistance. Researchers estimated an aggregate savings of $28,000 for each $5,000 spent on a child in the project ($3,000 reduced costs

associated with delinquency and crime; $5,000 savings in special
education and remedial school programs; $16,000 savings in pub-
lic assistance; $5,000 additional revenue in taxes collected be-
cause of better employment and earnings).[11]

Mere provision of funds for such opportunities for children
will not automatically produce results like these. Training both
leaders and teachers of such programs, as well as engaging the
cooperation of families of the children involved, takes time. The
idea that major positive results are easy is a myth. Serious work
over an extended period is required, but the example of Perry
shows that such work does bring effective results.

Self-esteem and motivation come much more easily to children who see genuine opportunities for themselves in American
society than they do to children living in circumstances that seem
hopeless. The Perry project is the best studied of the early
intervention programs, but many well-run Head Start programs
achieve similar results with their children. All children who live
in families falling below federal poverty guidelines are eligible
to participate in a Head Start program for one to two years before
starting kindergarten. For two decades less than 25 percent of
these eligible children have actually enrolled in Head Start programs, because the federal government has not appropriated
funds for the rest. In the first major increase in recent years,
Congress passed legislation in 1990 raising the appropriation for
Head Start so that approximately 40 percent of the eligible children can be served. This is a great improvement, but it still
leaves out in the cold a shocking 60 percent of the children for
whom the Head Start program was created. Again, this is an
example of the government knowing what it *should* do, but not
finding the political will to do it.[12]

The federal government needs to work in conjunction with
other governmental agencies, as well as with private voluntary
organizations, to revamp fundamentally its programs aimed at
fostering the healthy development of young people. While cooperation with other organizations is valuable, chiefly because
working on these issues successfully requires local commitment

and participation, nonetheless the primacy of the federal responsibility is clear. Our nation will not prosper if our children are not healthy. This is not a problem simply for inner-city Detroit or rural Alabama. It is a problem for the entire United States.

In 1990 Congress passed the Family and Medical Leave Act, which would have been a step toward better care for the nation's children. But President Bush vetoed the Act, after business groups expressed strong disapproval of its requirement that businesses with more than fifty employees grant up to three months of unpaid leave of absence to employees with a new child or an ill family member. The United States, therefore, remains with South Africa the only major industrialized nations that have no family leave legislation at all. Both Japan and West Germany mandate three months of paid leave as well as additional unpaid leave, and this policy does not seem to have inhibited their productivity.

In the United States we not only have no national policy of assistance in infancy and in illness but we also have no national policy of child care, despite the fact that most children live in families without any adult dedicated to their full-time care. Initiatives begun in the 1960s and 1970s to provide both care and standards for care declined in the 1980s, and currently an estimated 90 percent of home-based daycare operations in the United States are neither licensed nor monitored. Daycare is often provided by untrained, inexperienced, poorly paid workers; the turnover rate is 60 percent annually. Approximately 48 percent of American four-year-olds and 29 percent of three-year-olds participate in some kind of early childhood program to promote health, school readiness, and social skills along with supportive care. As with family leave, models from other countries show what can be done: in Belgium all four-year-olds and 95 percent of three-year-olds are in state-run nursery schools; 87 percent of Italian three-to-five-year-olds are in early childhood programs; Hong Kong has similar participation. In France 98 percent of three-to-five-year-olds attend free preschools that meet satisfactory standards of health, safety, and nurturance and are open from early morning to evening.[13] In urging South Carolina to be "first in first grade," Governor Riley was not even asking the people of his state to accomplish what many other nations have already achieved much more comprehensively.

Children who are not healthy will have special difficulties in school, and while it is the obligation of the public schools to do as well as they can with every child, healthy or not, assured and motivated or not, the schools are much more likely to be effective with children who come to them healthy, assured, and motivated. We know how to increase the proportion who come to school thus prepared, but we have not translated that knowledge into federally funded, well-managed programs that serve all who are eligible for them. In fact, we have crippled many successful programs in the 1980s by insufficiently funding them, and we have seen the effects: increases in number of children in poverty, more children without proper health care or immunizations, a decline in U.S. standing relative to other nations in terms of social, economic, and health status of our children. Fundamentally these are failings of our government, and the consequences of these failings are putting our future at risk. In the absence of appropriate governmental leadership, the schools are both hobbled in their efforts to educate all children well and subtly assured by the government that some children—ones who are poor and disproportionately ones who are minorities—need not be bothered about at all.

Education outside the Schools

While the federal responsibility for the operation of educational institutions such as schools and colleges is subsidiary to that of the states and local communities, the federal government has the primary responsibility in the domain of educational research and statistics. The impetus for the creation of the original Department of Education in 1867 was the need for fuller understanding of education throughout the United States, or as one of its supporters, Congressman Ignatius Donnelly, expressed it, the need to "illuminate the dark places of ignorance." The independent department was quickly downgraded to the status of an "Office" in the Department of the Interior in 1869 and in the following year was made a "Bureau." In 1929 the name changed back to the Office of Education, and ten years later it was relocated to the Federal Security Agency after spending seventy years in the Department of the Interior. That was its status when various disparate elements of the federal government, including the Social Security Administration and the National Institutes of Health, joined with it during the Eisenhower administration in 1953 to become the Department of Health, Education, and Welfare (HEW). Education was by far the smallest member of the triumvirate, which together by the 1970s had a budget equivalent to that of the sixth largest nation in the industrialized West.[14]

The major growth of the Office of Education occurred in the mid-1960s with the passage in 1965 of both the Elementary and Secondary Education Act (ESEA) and the Higher Education Act. Federal funding for elementary and secondary education roughly tripled in one year as spending increased from $891 million in 1965 to $2.4 billion in 1966.[15] For nearly a century the Office of Education had been a somnolent bureaucratic byway, but under the leadership of Francis Keppel and Harold Howe II from 1963 to 1969 it bustled with activity as it tried to send funds to school systems and states under ESEA and to college students and their campuses under the Higher Education Act. In the jargon of the times, the federal funds were to be used to "supplement, not supplant" the state and local funds already available to fund the educational operations. Although the fraction of federal funds available to local schools varied considerably, the national average at its peak in the 1970s was barely 12 percent of school budgets.

After the passage of the Civil Rights Act of 1964, the Office of Education also tried to desegregate both the public schools and the colleges and universities in the South. Its principal means was to threaten to withhold federal funds from districts that were segregated. In the end not much money was withheld, and the districts and institutions did desegregate, but the process was extremely labor-intensive and politically sensitive.

Through both these activities, its supplemental funding and its desegregation efforts, the Office of Education assisted other parts of government in accomplishing their aims. In the first instance it helped the states and local districts, which had the principal operational responsibility for schools and colleges. In the second instance it augmented the efforts of the Justice Department and the Supreme Court in hastening desegregation. In neither activity did the Office of Education have the leading responsibility.

But in a third area the Office of Education was not subordinate to any group and did have the primary responsibility in the nation. That was educational research. Just as education has been the third or fourth priority among the American people, so research has been the third or fourth priority among educators. If asked, most educators of the last generation would place increasing academic achievement, broadening educational access, and desegregating educational institutions before enhancing educational research. Thus, despite the century-old mandate to the federal government's education office to "illuminate the dark places of ignorance," its light was dim.

In the early 1970s, with Richard Nixon in the White House and a Democratically controlled Congress, the administration proposed that the existing Bureau of Educational Research within the Office of Education be eliminated and a separate and independent agency for educational research be created. It would be located within the Department of Health, Education, and Welfare and be structurally distinct from the Office of Education and administratively parallel to it. Models for it included the National Institutes of Health (NIH), already located within HEW, and the National Science Foundation (NSF), which was a free-standing agency with its own policy board in the executive branch of the government.

In 1972 the National Institute of Education (NIE) was created with its own policy board, the National Council on Educational Research, and a director who held the same rank as the Commissioner of Education and like the commissioner was appointed by the president, was confirmed by the Senate, and reported variously to the secretary of HEW or the assistant secretary for education. In short, NIE was a bureaucratic hybrid or mutant of NIH and NSF. Despite the best efforts of its two most visible supporters, John Brademas, a Democratic congressman from Indiana, and Daniel Patrick Moynihan, then a professor at Harvard on leave to the federal government, it never achieved the autonomy, funding, or support of either of its institutional precursors. Democrats accused the Republican administration of creating it in order to divert attention and funds from desegregation programs and aid to poor children. They called it a "Nixon trick." NIE never found the base of support in the Congress that it needed. Its first director entered the political legends by telling powerful Senator Warren Magnuson, chairman of the Appropriations Subcommittee on Labor, Health, Education, and Welfare, that he would prefer to attend an educational research meeting in Paris rather than testify before Senator Magnuson's committee, and by doing so. Senator Magnuson never forgot that example of political naïveté, and he threatened to eliminate all funding for NIE. Five years later, when I went as director of NIE to meet Senator Magnuson, the issue was still on his mind. Fortunately, he could tell the difference between me and my two male predecessors, and one of the new members of the National Council of Educational Research was a distinguished constituent and friend of his from Bellingham, Washington. He relented a bit, and did not actively oppose NIE.

Initially funded in 1972 at $140 million annually, NIE's budget shrank every year until 1977, by which time it had slumped to $70 million, much of which was committed in "setasides" for existing educational laboratories and research centers that had powerful lobbying in the Congress. In the first two years of the Carter administration its budget rose to nearly $100 million, but when the Department of Education was created in

1980, it was merged into the department and subsumed under the Office of Educational Research and Improvement, thereby losing its parallel equivalence with the operational Office of Education. When it was abolished by the Reagan administration, much of NIE's promise to do for education what NIH had done for health or NSF had done for science had been lost. A General Accounting Office study published in 1987 revealed that the federal educational research budget had been cut by nearly 80 percent in real dollars since the creation of NIE.[16] I know of no other federal agency that has suffered such massive budget cuts, when that federal agency has the leading responsibility in the nation for its kind of work.

The political constituency for educational research has always been elusive, depending heavily upon educational researchers themselves, who have often been their own worst enemy in arguing their case with the Congress. Their proclivity to be verbose, to qualify all findings, and to favor analysis of a problem over resolution of it has not won the hearts or minds of the members of Congress.

Educational researchers, unlike medical researchers, cannot promise any single-fix remedy to a life-threatening disease. There is no educational equivalent to a blocked coronary artery for which practitioners can utilize a research finding to provide an immediate restorative solution. The incentive for educators to rely upon research in order to be successful with their clients has always been more ambiguous than that for physicians. If research comes up with a better way to teach reading, for example, the new method is likely to take years to be implemented in the schools, and even when it has been adopted, its effectiveness may be hard to measure, and may not become clear for still more years. Advances in education do not save lives the way medical advances do, and it often is not easy to demonstrate just how much they enhance lives. Educational researchers, then, have difficulty finding practitioners who believe research is important either to the practitioner's or to the student's success.

Today two of the most important policy issues educators

debate, assessment of academic learning and school leadership, draw much of their intellectual power from work sponsored by NIE in the 1970s and early 1980s. Leaders in the assessment research, Lauren Resnick at the University of Pittsburgh's Learning Resources and Development Center and Lee Shulman, formerly at Michigan State University's Institute for Research on Teaching and now at Stanford University's School of Education, both were funded principally by NIE in the 1970s when they began their basic work on understanding how students and teachers learn. Similarly, much of the work illuminating the crucial leadership role of the school principal and the significance of school organization was undertaken in the late 1970s under the guidance of James March, a member of the National Council on Educational Research, and the administrative leadership of Marc Tucker and Fritz Mulhauser and their study group on school organization at NIE. The latter work has brought fundamental challenge to the reigning wisdom of James B. Conant that all children should attend large comprehensive high schools that can provide advanced placement courses for the few and a weakened general or vocational curriculum for the many. Conant's support for this type of high school was not based on research but rather on Conant's personal experience that such schools gave poor boys a better chance to get into Harvard.

Congress expects testimonials from satisfied clients for its programs, and in these days of immediate evaluation and accountability its patience for recognizing long-term benefits is thin. Nonetheless, it is worth noting that no important benefits in either agricultural or engineering research were realized until more than forty years after the passage of the original land grant legislation creating the Agricultural and Mechanical Arts universities. Justin B. Morrill had proposed those institutions as a way to improve agricultural and engineering productivity in America through research and training. Eventually the institutions did provide a base for vastly improved farm and industrial production, but it took them nearly half a century to show much result. In the meantime, the constituency of local congressmen continued to support these institutions for a more immediate and tangible outcome: federally funded higher education for citizens in their states. Today the land grant universities are research leaders in both agriculture and engineering, but it has also been 130 years since federal legislation created their faculties in those areas. NIE had no interim product that could win political support while the research developed. Nor were there any congressmen whose families were threatened by the educational equivalent of cancer or heart disease who would swing their support to NIE as they had to NIH.

The fact that educational researchers are poor public relations agents and that their results are not instantaneous does not mean, however, that the federal government should not support educational research. In education as in any other field progress and improvement come irregularly but persistently from the findings of research. To reduce or eliminate research in a field is extraordinarily short-sighted if one wishes to see gains in the field. Certainly the most successful American businesses understand this fundamental premise. In the words of David Kearns, the former chairman of Xerox, "No single feature of the education system is more shocking to business leaders than low levels of education research spending. We know more about pork bellies and soybean futures in this country than we do about our schools."[17] The federal government also recognizes the value of research in other domains to which it has given higher priority than education. For example, the Department of Defense's research budget for the Army alone is $5.2 billion; the entire research budget for the Department of Defense is over $36 billion; within the Department of Health and Human Services the budget for the National Institute of Child Health and Human Development is over $427 million; the research budget of the Department of Education is $85 million.[18] That is a shockingly low figure for a nation that says it wants to improve the education of its children and for a federal department that brought us *A Nation at Risk*. It is time for the feds to fund educational research.

In addition to educational research, there are a number of other federal programs that contribute to children's education. For example, public libraries in local communities are vastly underfunded, and the federal government currently provides only $132 million per year in support, most of it to school libraries. Children constitute about 40 percent of public library users, but more than half the libraries in the country have no librarian who works specifically with children. Museums, both specialized ones such as science or children's museums and broader art ones, offer many opportunities for children, but relatively few children benefit from them. The entire federal appropriation for the Institute for Museum Services at present is $22.7 million.[19] Similarly, the National Endowment for the Humanities, the National Endowment for the Arts, and the National Science Foundation have modest programs dealing with children's learning of the humanities, arts, and sciences. The total for all those programs is less than $270 million, with the great bulk devoted to the Science Education Directorate, which encompasses many projects besides children's science. The elementary and secondary education program for the arts, for instance, is only $6.5 million, while for all the humanities it is just $7.5 million. The focus of all these agencies is upon adults, whom the federal government has considered to be more important recipients of government attention than children. That assumption must be challenged. It is based primarily on the fact that adults vote and children do not. It is not based on either needs or national interest.[20]

A third and vital way in which the federal government can assist educational activities outside the schools is through the regulatory process. Unlike the previous examples and many of the subsequent ones, this does not cost money. It does require political clout, a commodity often in even shorter supply for worthy causes than money. An example of such a shortage was the death of the Children's Television Act of 1988, despite bipartisan support in Congress including unanimous passage by the Senate, because President Reagan refused to sign it. That legislation would have required television stations to consider the welfare and needs of children in their programming, a requirement that recent FCC rulings have eliminated and something that many stations did not want to do. In 1990 the Congress again passed a similar bill, and President Bush let it become law without his signature. This law limits the amount of advertising that can be shown on children's programs to 10½ minutes per hour on weekends and 12 minutes per hour on weekdays, thus putting a limit on advertising that has grown substantially since the advent of deregulation in 1984. Since children, particularly ones from low-income families, spend enormous amounts of time in front of TV sets, changes in programming could benefit them immensely. Current estimates suggest that children spend more time watching television than they do in school, and will have been exposed to 200,000 commercials by the time they are eighteen.[21]

As discussed in Chapter 2, families would benefit greatly from federal regulatory changes that would provide incentives to integrate the efforts of the many federal, state, and local agencies that now provide children's services. The health services are separate from the welfare ones, which remain isolated from the educational ones, which are frequently distant from the food supports. Daycare and employment services are distinct from each other and from the others. Yet a poor mother struggling to get on her feet economically needs all these services for herself and her children. Current regulatory Balkanization makes it extremely difficult for her either to understand or to benefit from the programs for which she is eligible. Undoubtedly there is no magic solution to the regulatory maze, but much more creative experimentation should be tried.

Current efforts in Dayton, Little Rock, Savannah, and Pittsburgh, supported by the Annie P. Casey Foundation, are examples of communities attempting to find their way through the maze and provide more user-friendly services. These cities have implemented collaborative community plans to identify and remove barriers in each city's helping system and to create a network of support for youth that permits caseworkers to knit together comprehensive programs to provide services to decrease high school dropout rates, teenage pregnancy, and youth unemployment.

One very positive long-term development on this front is the shift in emphasis within the General Accounting Office from traditional fiscal accounting approaches to broader program evaluations. Many recipients of federal funds have tailored their programs to meet auditing requirements to be sure they would not be subject to allegations of fraud. Such tailoring frequently benefited the people who ran the programs more than the people who were supposed to be receiving their services.

A common example of such tailoring is the practice, followed by many school systems that use Title I funds for supplementary reading instruction, of having children who are eligible for Title I leave their regular classrooms for the additional instruction. This process is known as "pull-out," and it allows the district to show that the federal funds have been used only on eligible children and for the designated purpose. Thus, it makes a very clear audit trail, assuring the feds that the money was spent on the right children for the right services. The educational consequences for the children, however, are often negative. First, they are stigmatized by their removal as being either dumb or poor or both, and secondly, they may be missing something very important in their regular class. Since the overall point of the legislation is to improve the children's education, not to facilitate auditing, federal education officials have regularly decried "pull-out," insisting that it is not required, but administrators, who remain hassled by auditors, persist in the practice, putting their own convenience above children's educational needs.

Aiding School Reform

As we entered the 1990s, federal activity in education shifted from popular booklets decrying the schooling of our children (*A Nation at Risk*, 1983) to highminded, broad, but low-cost discussions about national goals in education (*America 2000*, 1991). George Bush pronounced himself an "education president," but thus far, his record is much stronger on rhetoric than in reality. Not until mid-1991, barely a year before the election, did he assemble his new leadership for the Department of Education.[22]

An earlier Texan in the White House, Lyndon B. Johnson, also aspired to be an "education president" and actually was one. He supported legislation, programs, and regulations that brought about federally supported preschool programs, federal aid to elementary and secondary schools, significant increases in college attendance, desegregation of southern schools, reductions in poverty, and improvements in health. His successors have not maintained that momentum. Their métier has been high-minded talk about school reform, leaving the hard work of implementation to state and local officials to work out as they might.

The 1980s, in particular, were a low point in the federal government's efforts for education in general and for schools in particular. The House of Representatives lost its leading Republican and Democratic spokesmen for education, Albert Quie from Minnesota and John Brademas from Indiana, when their districts refused to return them to Congress in 1978 and in 1980, respectively. The new Department of Education, created by President Carter in the spring of 1980 shortly before he was defeated in the election in November, did not have adequate time to launch major initiatives. The choice of Shirley Hufstedtler, a distinguished lawyer but not an educator, as the first Secretary of Education did little to indicate that education was high on the national agenda.

The Reagan years gave us the spectacle of infighting within the Department of Education between those employees who wanted to fulfill the new president's promise to abolish the department and those who wanted to save it. Many of the best civil servants left the department, believing they could better serve their government and their country in the General Accounting Office or elsewhere.

With the arrival of William Bennett as Secretary of Education in 1985, educational rhetoric escalated, but the guiding ideology of privatization and decreased public spending on domestic issues prevailed. Bennett and his indomitable assistant Chester Finn laid the basis for the ensuing focus of discussion on national educational goals to be implemented by state and local authorities, both public and private, with only words of admonition and occasional encouragement from Washington. In the fall of 1989 the president held an Education Summit with the nation's governors, and they declared, "the time has come, for the first time in U.S. history, to establish clear, national performance goals, goals that will make us internationally competitive." Economic rivalry with other nations, not the benefits of learning for our children, seemed to be the stimulus. They announced six such national goals:

1. By the year 2000, all children in America will start schools ready to learn.
2. By the year 2000, we will increase the percentage of students graduating from high school to at least 90%.
3. By the year 2000, American students will leave grades four, eight, and twelve having demonstrated competency over challenging subject matter, including English, mathematics, science, history, and geography.
4. By the year 2000, U.S. students will be first in the world in science and mathematics achievement.
5. By the year 2000, every adult American will be literate and possess the knowledge and skills necessary to compete in a global economy and exercise the rights and responsibilities of citizenship.
6. By the year 2000, every school in America will be free of drugs and violence and offer a disciplined environment conducive to learning.[23]

Since these goals were announced, the largest percentage increase in the Department of Education budget has been for the Center for Education Statistics, which is ably managed by a longtime civil servant, Emerson Elliott. The Center funds the National Assessment of Educational Progress, which will tell us whether we are meeting the goals. No comparable increases have been sought to improve training programs for teachers or administrators to aid them in meeting these goals, or for health or antipoverty programs for children to help them arrive at school more in the mood to learn. Increased testing and discussion of national standards are highly visible and relatively low-cost approaches to a genuinely difficult and complex problem: improving the academic achievement of the young.

Both high visibility and low cost are desirable characteristics to politicians who wish to demonstrate concern about the problem but who do not wish to levy new taxes for more expensive solutions. After a decade or two of being ignored, some educators are so pleased to be back in the public debate that they are hesitant to criticize proposed solutions that are popular with government officials and the newly sensitized business community. In holding their tongues, the educators may seem to be agreeing with solutions that all their sensible colleagues know will not work. Simply raising the standard without improving the school's capacity to teach will not result in more students achieving that standard. The preparation of the students must be enhanced, and the government has a responsibility to aid in that enhancement as well as to enunciate goals. Concretely, the federal government can stimulate school reform in several different ways. A discussion of these ways follows.

Regulatory Relief

Nowhere is the regulatory thicket more dense than in the world of public schools. The schools now receive less than 8 percent of their funding from the federal government, but most school people would contend that they spend considerably more than 8 percent of their administrative time on conforming to the regulations that come with the money.[24] Hence, the dictum of simplified and integrated regulation is particularly appropriate for the public schools. Their future success undoubtedly rests on devising new ways in which the academic learning expected in the school can be incorporated into a broader function being served by the school building. The building must provide a location for a variety of nonacademic services needed by the students and their families, as well as maintaining its traditional academic program. In some high schools, for example, I am sure that the best single step to take to boost test scores would be the installation of a daycare facility for the children of the student mothers who now attend only intermittently. Teenage mothers are concerned about the care of their babies, and most pay greater attention to their children's needs, which are certainly more immediate, than they do to their own, which can be deferred. Educational needs are the most likely to be deferred, particularly when the young mother has no safe place to leave her baby during the school day, and therefore stays home with it. Both she and her baby will suffer in the long run if she does not receive the education that will allow her to realize her full gifts and to be a productive member of society.

For most burdened school people, even though they recognize that rationality would dictate that their building serve many purposes other than instruction in academic subjects, the regulatory obstacles are simply too great to be overcome. Federal regulations are not the only ones with which the school people must deal, but if federal leadership means anything, it is the federal government that can provide the initial effort in attempting to simplify the bureaucratic hurdles to providing integrated services to children through the school building. Such efforts will not be costly and ultimately may even save some public funds.

Other federal programs to improve the schools will cost money. I am not suggesting that we overthrow our traditional mode of the primary financing of our schools, which is through state and local governments. But the problems of poverty, productivity, participation, and passivity are not ones that are located solely in Michigan, Missouri, or Montana. They are national ones that affect all of us in the United States, and therefore there is a federal imperative to address the issues through public schools. Two kinds of federal help to the schools are essential: expansion of Chapter I so that all eligible children can be served, and development of model programs to serve particular national needs.

Chapter I

Chapter I has evolved from Title I of the Elementary and Secondary Education Act of 1965. The original Title I provided funds to school districts with high concentrations of poor children on the assumption that such children needed special help in school in order to do well in their academic subjects, an assumption that has not been challenged.

The program was authorized for all twelve school grades, but because there were never sufficient funds appropriated to fund it fully, its efforts were concentrated on the early grades, where prevention of learning problems might occur and where the learning expected was better understood than that in the higher grades. Like most early evaluations of complex social programs, the initial studies of Title I found its results mixed at best, but by 1977 an evaluation by the National Institute of Education, commissioned by the Congress, revealed that in well-managed programs children made real gains in reading and arithmetic. Despite these and other positive findings, Congress has not substantially increased the appropriations for the program, and it currently serves fewer than half of the eligible children. In particular, the program has remained concentrated in the elementary years, and it has rarely been extended to high school, the point in the educational process where American children most clearly perform less well than children in many other countries. Chapter I is currently funded at $6.2 billion.[25]

Model Programs

Just as local communities and states inaugurate new programs to meet particular needs, so should the federal government undertake efforts to address large national issues in education. Let me suggest four specific educational issues that could be addressed by model federal programs. They exemplify initiatives the federal government should undertake.

Issue: By the end of the century it is estimated that between 30 and 40 percent of schoolchildren will be from minority groups, yet the current percentage of minority teachers is less than 10 percent and dropping.

Model program: Create scholarships in one-year teacher education programs for members of minority groups who will then have an obligation to enter public school teaching for at least three years; 500 such scholarships at $15,000 per student would cost $7,500,000 annually.

Issue: By the end of the century it is estimated that approximately half of the present public school teachers will retire or quit, thus creating an acute shortage of teachers.

Model program: Create scholarships in one-year teacher education programs for persons who will then have an obligation to enter public school teaching for at least three years; 1,000 scholarships per year at $15,000 per student would cost $15,000,000 annually.

Issue: Most experienced teachers and administrators have no funded opportunities for additional study once they have completed their certification; given their salaries, few can pay for it themselves. Yet those in difficult or poor schools have particular need for the professional revitalization provided by full-time study.

Model program: Grant sabbaticals for graduate study in their fields for teachers and administrators in schools with predominantly poor student bodies or in schools below the state average in per-pupil expenditure; 500 sabbaticals per year at $30,000 per person would cost $15,000,000 annually.

Issue: Many large school systems are currently considering implementing "school site management," but few have any experience with giving significant managerial responsibility to mid-level administrators, as such changes would require.

Model program: Grant sabbaticals and summer fellowships for such prospective school site managers; 250 sabbaticals per year at $30,000 each would cost $7,500,000 annually, and 1,000 summer fellowships per year at $5,000 each, $5,000,000.

These remedies would cost a total of $50 million annually. That is only 0.2 percent of the current budget of the Department of Education, and this sum would be less than nine days of interest payments alone on the government's savings and loan bail-out. Surely the improvement of our children's schooling and our national future is worth that much.

· 4 ·

Higher Education

In Atlanta, faculty and administrators at Clark University and Spelman College are developing programs to link their historically black institutions more closely to the communities around them. Graduate students in social work and education at Clark are living in a public housing project in order to understand better the circumstances of their clients' and students' lives. Within the project the Clark contingent organizes education, job training, and child care programs for the other residents. Spelman College, Clark's sister institution in the Atlanta University consortium, is planning similar kinds of outreach activities under the leadership of its president, Johnetta Cole, and its new faculty appointee, Alonzo Crim, the former Atlanta superintendent of schools.[1]

These new programs are examples of the kinds of cooperation and coordination that are beginning to occur between institutions of higher education and the communities around them. In 1979 Yale University, which does not have a school of education, organized a Yale–New Haven Teachers Institute to provide seminars for local school teachers with Yale faculty to pursue common academic interests. More than a decade ago Stanford University initiated a series of cooperative projects with its neighboring school districts under the leadership of its then president, Donald Kennedy, and the dean of its school of education at the time, J. Myron Atkin.

Throughout the nation there are many individual programs linking colleges and universities with schools. Most of these are paid for with foundation grants or other outside sources, and few are institutionalized into the central mission of the institutions or into their core budgets. Nonetheless, the many examples, which in the Boston area range from Boston University's contract to run the school system in the neighboring city of Chelsea to the Harvard Graduate School of Education's collaborative partnership with Boston English High School, illustrate that on nearly every college campus in America there is some involvement with the local schools. The potential exists for cooperation in myriad ways, but it has not yet been realized. Why not?

One of the most deeply suppressed truths in America is that elementary/secondary education and higher education are part of the same enterprise. The possibility has not even occurred to many university people. School people often yearn for a connection through their Advanced Placement courses but recognize that their legitimacy in the college/university world is severely limited. Higher education folk, if asked, can explain how their world differs from that of school people: they seek to discover and to advance new knowledge; they select their clientele and ostensibly admit only those who are qualified; they deal with young adults, the future leaders of the society, not children with diverse destinies.

Other differences, less likely to be cited but probably at least as important in maintaining the cultural chasm between the two types of institutions, are that higher education faculty and administrators are clearly professionals in America, while elementary/secondary ones are considered only marginally so; that particularly in the most prestigious colleges and universities, faculties enjoy a high degree of autonomy from administrators, while in many schools administrators and union contracts combine to regulate teachers' behavior closely; and finally, and most important culturally, that men predominate in colleges and universities, particularly in positions of responsibility (full professors and senior administrators), while women overwhelmingly predominate in the schools, except in the most senior administrative positions.

In short, higher education is men's work and schooling is women's work; the former deals with elite young adults, the latter with all children. The society values the former and does not value the latter. The United States is considered preeminent internationally in its universities, but its schools have not been considered so since the 1940s. No wonder that the higher education community wishes to maintain its distance from the troublesome world of schools.

Today many in higher education are recognizing, albeit reluctantly, that elementary/secondary and higher education are not separate entities but parts of a continuum. Most college and university people know that, in fact, it is only a minority of the professors who are discovering and advancing new knowledge. The existence of such a group is terribly important and must be maintained, but it is not a group in which most faculty members participate. Instead of pushing at the boundaries of knowledge, most are trying to help students understand old knowledge leavened with a little recent, but not new, knowledge.

The battles over curriculum in the humanities and social sciences on college campuses in the past two decades have rarely been about new knowledge. Rather, they have been about interpretation: What has distinction? What is important? Today the focus is upon new groups and new questions, upon issues of which groups' experiences should be preserved, taught, and examined, and what the legitimate and appropriate methodologies are for doing so. By investigating new groups and by asking new questions we fundamentally change our understanding of both our past and our present, of our history and our culture. Should the writings of blacks or Hispanics have a place in the curriculum, and should they dislodge other works? The argument often rests on what the disputants believe is the "distinc-

tion" of the texts, and on such matters, there is frequent
disagreement. Should women's experiences occupy significant
parts of the curriculum? Here the discussion focuses usually not
on "distinction" but on the "importance" of women's perceptions
and lives. On this matter, too, many disagree. Are the traditions,
attitudes, and daily life of ordinary people and of identifiable
racial, ethnic, or religious groups grist for the curricular mill?
Do we need to know about the experience of Roman Catholic,
Italian immigrant women in Buffalo, preferably in their own
words, or is our traditional understanding of religion, immigra-
tion, and local politics enough? The president of the Modern
Language Association, Catharine R. Stimpson, urged in her 1990
presidential address that we need both.

These discussions are quite different from the legendary fight
between science and religion in the nineteenth century triggered
by the teaching of evolutionary theory. That disagreement rested
on the discovery of new knowledge that questioned many religious interpretations, including the place of humans in the
universe. The current debates do not involve much religious
dispute, but they arouse intense secular controversy. These debates raise questions not about the place of humans in the universe but, rather, about individuals' understanding of their own
and their culture's role in society. What experiences and cultures
have both distinction and importance? In the secular environment in which most colleges and universities exist today, such
issues are just as fractious and divisive as evolution was more
than a century ago. These questions are also at the heart of many
debates about the role of multicultural education at the elementary and secondary level, and hence are an example of an
issue in which higher education faculty share a common concern,
albeit often unknowingly, with school teachers.

The other differences cited by higher education folk as evidence of their separateness from school people can be rebutted
as well: only a very small number of colleges and universities
are really selective in their admissions policies; most accept most
applicants, at least from their own states. Furthermore, under-

graduate populations are not as young as they used to be; many institutions that faced enrollment crises in the 1980s have been saved from dangerous underenrollment by an increase in the ranks of older (over twenty-five) undergraduates, most of them women. These older students now make up 40 percent of the undergraduate student bodies, and although they are often very good students, they are much less likely to be in the vanguard of society's new leaders than are the twenty-year-old white males traditionally favored by the colleges.[2] In short, undergraduates are coming much closer to representing the diversity of the American population, as do elementary and secondary students.

College and university faculties are selecting more women, and while there are still great disparities between the three-quarters of teachers who are women and the two-fifths of college faculty who are, the split is narrowing. The gap remains most notable in senior faculty positions at major universities, which still rarely have even 12 percent women in most departments. The proportions of school superintendents and college presidents who are women are roughly comparable at about 5 percent and 10 percent, respectively.[3]

Talking with Each Other

These indications of growing similarity with their fellow educators in the elementary/secondary sector may not be apparent to most university faculty members, but at least some in the professoriat and many in college and university administrations, who are paid to worry about such matters, have come to see that the schools are in trouble and that the colleges and universities may need to do something about it. Higher education is not only recognizing its increasing professional solidarity with the schools around a common educational mission, but also realizing how much colleges and universities depend on having the schools produce enough high school graduates who can and will undertake college work. Since the numbers of eighteen-year-olds began to decline a decade ago, the colleges have become more attentive. For too long, the cultural and social differences between higher education and elementary/secondary education have obscured the powerful self-interest that the colleges have in developing a close and congenial relationship with the high schools.

The traditional way in which colleges and universities have maintained their relationship with the schools is through their admissions offices. These places are populated with individuals, often recent graduates of the institution, who travel to high schools that have promising candidates and entreat the students to apply to their colleges. The staff of the admissions office typically is utterly separate from the faculty of the institution and equally remote from curricular expectations of the departments.

One organization in America, the College Board, regularly brings together high school counselors and teachers with college admissions officers, but generally not with college or university faculty. In its best-known function the College Board provides the Scholastic Aptitude Test (SAT) to about 40 percent of the high school seniors annually.[4] The Board also creates one of the few occasions for secondary and higher education people to gather to discuss common issues. As one might suspect, however, those in attendance at such meetings often represent disproportionately those school people with an orientation to placing their graduates in the minority of U.S. colleges that require the College Board tests for admission. The meetings are valuable, but they do not provide the broad consideration of the links between school and college that is needed.

All college admissions officers recognize that they are judged by the class they bring in, by its size and by its quality. In most institutions the first issue is more pressing than the second. Since the budget of most colleges is heavily determined either by the tuition received from students or by the funds appropriated by the legislature, which are based upon enrollment figures, the number of enrollees is vitally important. In the early twentieth century it was quite common for colleges to maintain a preparatory department for those students judged not fully prepared to undertake college work. Today we call that remediation, and we often give college credit for such courses. It is virtually unknown for a college today to have students on campus in a "prep" program, although many college faculty complain about inadequate academic preparation of their students. In many colleges the kind of high school curriculum—college preparatory, general, or even vocational—completed in high school does not matter for admission. Only the diploma and perhaps the grades received determine eligibility for college.

One major university in America is trying to change this. The City University of New York (CUNY), with its eighteen undergraduate colleges, has announced that beginning in the fall of 1992 it will require completion of a high school college preparatory curriculum, as well as a college curriculum, before permitting students to graduate. Thus CUNY has both maintained its commitment to open enrollment (accepting high school graduates without regard to what course of studies they undertook in high school or how well they did in them) and reasserted its commitment to academic learning. Presumably those high school graduates who have not completed a traditional college prep high school course (four years of English, two years of laboratory science, a foreign language, history or social studies, algebra, geometry, and trigonometry) will enroll in such courses at their CUNY college along with regular college studies. It may take them more than four years to graduate from CUNY. At present only 20 percent of New York City high school graduates receive a "Regents-endorsed diploma," which certifies that they have completed a college prep curriculum and passed exams in those subjects. Currently more than 70 percent of the New York City high school graduates apply to CUNY, and slightly less than 50 percent enroll. Ann Reynolds, the chancellor of the CUNY system, proposed this new plan, which presumably will both strengthen the CUNY courses and push New York City high schools to encourage more students to take a college prep course. Such a curriculum, many would argue, is good preparation not

only for college but also for life, since it is more likely to engage
student and teacher in serious reading, writing, thinking, and
quantitative reasoning than either a vocational or a general
course.[5] To paraphrase General Motors CEO Charles Wilson's
mid-century comment about his company, "What's good for
CUNY is good for the country."

Most faculties have not been as thoughtful as CUNY about
simultaneously maintaining their enrollment and raising their
academic standards. It is more common for professors, when
asked about the problems of the schools and their manifestation
on their campuses, simply to suggest raising the college admissions requirements, without giving much attention to the source
of these tuition-paying students. Such a view begs the question
about the role the college and university community could or
should play in actually improving the schools and suggests that
university people wish to remain in pristine isolation from the
problems encountered by their fellow educators in the schools.
It also implies a belief that the relatively few institutions that
do have explicit, substantive requirements exert such an influence in American education that changes in their admissions
requirements would influence American elementary and secondary schools as a whole. The efforts of the CUNY system,
with its open enrollment policy, to devise a way to attack this
problem in our largest city are admirable. They should be widely
emulated by other institutions and adapted to their local circumstances.

Underneath the professor's easily criticized clarion call simply to raise admissions requirements lies the reality that most
colleges and universities have been so concerned with either
the quantity or the quality of their applicant pools that they have
not considered both issues together. CUNY is the exception,
not the rule. In 1892 when Charles William Eliot, the president
of Harvard University, chaired the National Education Association's Committee of Ten to recommend changes in the high
school curriculum, his chairmanship gave credibility to the principle that college people knew what the young must study in

high school if they were to succeed in college. Further, the NEA believed that a collaborative committee of school and college people under its auspices could influence in important ways what the high schools taught. In recent years, however, there has been very little joint discussion between school and college folk interested in instruction or curriculum. What many schools have concluded from these changes is that colleges no longer seem to care what their applicants study in high school, and the inference that schools have often made is that they are free to take the path of least resistance and offer a high school curriculum that appeals either to the student or to the teacher and need not effectively prepare students for college or anything else.

As the CUNY example indicates, there is a role for colleges to establish their admissions requirements as both symbolic and tangible expressions of what higher education believes that eighteen-year-olds entering its institutions should know. Such requirements should not be so onerous that poorly financed schools cannot provide them for their students, but the typical pre-college curriculum that CUNY suggests is neither fiscally nor intellectually confining for either college-bound or non-college-bound students. Yet such a curriculum is followed today by only a minority of high school students.

Colleges have a vital role to play in this matter. While clearly agreement about the names of the courses is helpful, even more important is agreement about the content. What is described as U.S. History in one school district may have little resemblance to it somewhere else. I do not mean that uniformity of coverage should be the goal, but rather that discussion between school and college people about what critical historical experiences and insights students should acquire would be helpful. For example, most university professors probably are not concerned that high school students be able to recite the date of Abraham Lincoln's Emancipation Proclamation or of Andrew Johnson's impeachment, but they would like students to know the relationship between Reconstruction and the Jim Crow Era. College admissions officers could play important brokering roles in organizing these conversations, but the principals in them should be the faculty members responsible for undergraduate instruction in their departments and supporting administrators joined by their counterparts in the schools. Such conversations could be very fruitful, exposing each group to the realities of the other's circumstances, and might result in some important changes in both high school and college teaching. In setting up meetings to make these conversations possible, one vital role for the admissions officers is to ensure that a broad range of high schools are represented, both ones from which the college typically draws applicants and ones from which it would like to draw.

Besides recognizing their common educational enterprise with the schools and establishing a closer relationship with them, the higher education community can contribute in three important ways in improving the schools: by increasing our understanding of student learning, by supporting applications of knowledge, and by strengthening schools of education.

Understanding Student Learning

Instruction in higher education tends to be of the take-it-or-leave-it variety. In graduate seminars with dedicated aspiring professionals whose motivation for learning the material is high and whose preparation in the subject is considerable, such a mode is probably effective. But for undergraduates with widely disparate backgrounds and levels of interest in the subject, it is not. Colleges and universities give relatively little attention to issues of instruction, and if they come up at all, the focus is usually on either curriculum or teaching, subjects of greater interest to the faculty than learning. The point, however, is student learning.

The first focus is usually on curricular requirements, that is, what subjects are to be taught and what fraction should be required for which majors. Should there be one or two years of laboratory science? Should there be a social science requirement, or should students be required to take specific courses in political science, economics, or sociology? Much faculty energy can be dissipated on such discussions, which often have a great deal more to do with political arrangements among departments than with differing perceptions of academic priorities. The second focus is typically on modes of instruction, such as size of classes, use of teaching assistants or computers, lectures versus discussions, relative roles of senior faculty and graduate assistants, amount of laboratory time required.

Both curricular content and modes of instruction are at the heart of professors' concerns. But student learning, while influenced by both curriculum and pedagogical styles, is not a direct function of either, and an investigation of these is only tangential to an understanding of student learning. The point of education is student learning, not settling political scores of professors. The more we know about how students learn and what helps them do so, the better education we will be able to give them.

Colleges and universities have within their faculties and administrations substantial resources for investigating such matters. Questions about learning relate to key issues in psychology, sociology, anthropology, and education. Yet the application of these researchable questions to college or school practice has been very limited. Scholars prefer to investigate psychological, social, cultural, or educational phenomena at greater distance from their own workplace. When the work applies to one's own university, it is called "institutional research," which by convention means that it has less prestige and, therefore, is pursued by less prestigious individuals than are investigations at more distant sites. Studying higher education in the Soviet Union is appropriate for a specialist in Soviet affairs, a high-status calling, while analysis of higher education in America may be appropriate for an administrator or a school of education faculty member, both lower in the pecking order at research universities than senior faculty members in the arts and sciences. Study of one's own university is typically undertaken by the staff of an obscure administrative office. This tradition, while changing some today, affects the quality of what we know about educational organization and instruction, and thus limits the usefulness of college and university people to elementary and secondary ones.

Were institutions of higher education to investigate seriously the learning of their students and to sort out the relative influences of peer culture, personal motivation, background knowledge, and various pedagogies, they would make an immense contribution that could help the schools. One such investigation has been pursued for the past several years by faculty and administrators at a number of New England colleges, led by Richard J. Light of Harvard University. Among their findings are the value of the one-minute paper (an idea developed by K. Patricia Cross of the University of California at Berkeley) to assess what students find most helpful or least clear in a class session, and ways to increase girls' oral participation in classes, especially ones in which they are in the minority.[6] Investigations of student learning of these kinds can have great utility for school people in their work.

In spite of growing efforts to assess and enhance student learning on many campuses, the gulf between examining student learning and engaging in academic research remains great. Only rarely are both seen as valuable faculty contributions. The pressure in most higher educational institutions today, rightly or wrongly, is to do more research, and investigations of how students learn are not, for some reason, counted as research in this sense. Meanwhile, school teachers are caught in the frenzy of testing triggered by the educational reforms of the 1980s. What the elementary and secondary school faculty need are some broader modes of assessing student progress and some more imaginative curricular and pedagogic strategies to enhance learning. College faculty need those too, and common cause could be made around questions of curriculum, pedagogy, and assessment.

Currently some of the most effective learning of which I am aware takes place at the Harvard Business School, where clarity about its goal—training general managers for companies—drives both the organization of instruction and the culture of the institution. There teachers offering different sections of the same course regularly meet to discuss pedagogical strategies, to share teaching notes, or to consider refinements to the curriculum. For the faculty these are some of their most important professional encounters. They are not wildly expensive, but they are very important. The goal also drives the school's admissions policy, a luxury many institutions do not have. Most institutions of higher education lack such clarity about why the students are enrolled and certainly do not consciously organize institutional life around it. Were they to do so and to make explicit their commitment to, say, a liberal arts education or professional preparation in a particular field, such as nursing, then the benefits of such focus might well be observed in their programs. While most institutions do not have the financial resources of the Harvard Business School, the principle of clear organizational focus is applicable in many settings. It is the basis, for example, of the magnet school movement currently in vogue in many cities, in which schools develop a particular focus, such as science, the arts, or music. A clearer articulation of the principle and of its applicability in a variety of settings would be a genuine contribution of higher education to the elementary/secondary policy discussions.

Throughout colleges and universities are outstanding teachers, typically rewarded with local reputations and occasional recognition by student election as winners of the "best teacher award." My father received one of these awards in the mid-1950s, and his name can still be found dimly etched on a plaque on the second floor of the Purdue University Memorial Student Union. He was pleased by the student selection, but he received no notice—fiscal or otherwise—from the Purdue administration of this honor. Stanford's former president, Donald Kennedy, wanted to change the reward system for university teaching, and announced a new $7 million program to do so.

Sometimes the winners of such awards are junior faculty who do not get tenure, and a modest student protest occurs. Often, though, they are experienced, senior faculty with a deep com-

mitment both to the institution and to the learning of the students. Rarely are they ever asked to tap their extraordinary
reservoir of knowledge and talent and to become what Donald
Schon terms "the reflective practitioner," and to aid others seeking to become more effective enhancers of student learning.[7]

Such assistance from these "reflective practitioners" could
be tremendously valuable both for the college or university's
efforts to enhance the learning of its students and for its own
understanding of how that learning occurs. As Schon has observed, professional practice, in this case college teaching, is
both learnable and coachable but not teachable.[8] Some of those
"best teachers" could become the reflective practitioners who
might move our knowledge of teaching and learning beyond
science to wisdom. By working with other faculty to improve
their teaching, either by coaching them directly or by team
teaching with them (indirect coaching by example) such adept
teachers could assist their colleagues and enhance student learning. The culture of the institution, though, must support such
activities, and many currently do not.

Many factors influence student learning, and while formal
instruction in classrooms is certainly among them, one important
contribution of higher education to the schools would be assistance both in analyzing the factors that enhance student learning
and in changing practices so that learning is more likely to occur.
Of the two assignments, analyzing the factors will probably be
easier for the universities than changing the practices. Explaining, not changing, is the university's expertise.

Supporting Applications of Knowledge

Using knowledge to enhance the healthy development and education of children requires not only fundamental conceptual
breakthroughs in cognition but also much intensive labor applying what we already know in diverse settings and in varied
ways. The fact that scientists have developed in their laboratories
an effective vaccine against polio does not prevent a polio epi-

demic unless that vaccine is injected into the arms of all children. Getting the vaccine from the laboratory to all the arms is at least as difficult as developing the vaccine in the first place. Yet within academe the development of the vaccine has substantially higher status than its distribution. If colleges and universities are to be helpful in solving the educational dilemmas of the schools, then they will need to develop more support on their own campuses for applications of knowledge.

Traditionally the American college and university community has valued basic research over applied research. We have Nobel Prizes for fundamental contributions, but we have few comparable awards for those who have taken good ideas and made them work well in new human settings. Academics find it much more appealing to try to think up a new idea than to apply that idea to the solution of a problem of the real world. The issues of analysis are much more compelling than the issues of implementation. Professors prefer to define the problem correctly and leave its resolution to someone else. But both analysis and implementation, definition and resolution, are necessary if knowledge is to lead to solutions for real-world problems.

The hierarchy of our leading universities reflects this preference for basic research. When a professional school, such as a school of public health or education, seeks to hire economists or historians to bring their disciplinary specialty to the service of the profession, the assumption is often made that such a scholar is leaving his or her principal calling and doing inferior work in trying to understand and to improve health care or schooling in America.

Both basic and applied knowledge are important, and the argument here is not against basic research. Rather, it is against the unitary importance accorded basic research within the university setting. As long as applications of research are undervalued in universities, the higher education community will not be eager to cooperate in a serious way with schools to assist them.

The problems that are most pressing both in the United

States and in the world are ones that require applied knowledge, particularly knowledge of how to get human beings to work together more constructively. It is unlikely that the American problems of poverty, productivity, public participation, and personal passivity will be solved by breakthroughs in fundamental research, although it is possible that problem-focused research activities—in the humanities, the social and behavioral sciences, engineering, public health, medicine, public policy, education, law, and business—could do much to ameliorate them. The reduction of international problems in the Middle East or Africa, for example, requires much that is currently available in the university, from a thorough historical and cultural knowledge of the societies in question to skill in negotiation and conflict resolution. While the function of institutions of higher education is not simply to solve broad social problems, so long as the institutions exist with public support they must include such broad social considerations on their agenda. Ever since Benjamin Franklin raised the question more than two hundred years ago, we have pondered the relative value of useful and ornamental knowledge. We have always believed there is a place for both.

In times of crisis university scholars have often come together off-campus to address particularly vexing problems in effective ways. Probably the best-known example of collaborative scholarship to solve a technical problem in this century is the Manhattan Project, in which scientists from several leading universities, mostly physicists, worked together to supervise the design and construction of the atomic bomb so that the Allies could defeat Japan and Germany and win World War II. Many people have had second thoughts about atomic weaponry since then, but at the time this was strongly believed to be physics in the nation's service. Similarly, Franklin Delano Roosevelt had brought his Brain Trust of university scholars to Washington to help him and the government officials already there to devise and implement the New Deal. Also during World War II university faculty members and aspiring academics populated a number of crucial government agencies, particularly the Office of Strategic Services (precursor to the Central Intelligence

Agency, which has not been a haven for university-based academics). During World War I a group of leading psychologists from universities throughout the United States, led by Robert Yerkes of Harvard, conceived and administered the first group intelligence tests, known as the Army Alpha and Beta.

All these are examples of scholars leaving the halls of academe and applying their knowledge in different settings. The practice continues of recruiting from all levels of academe for service in the government, where expertise will be applied to problems of the real world. Advising companies is common among business school faculty members, so widespread among some that such consulting is the bane of many deans' existence since it distracts professors from their duties to the university. Law professors sometimes have private practices that also are highly paid and visible and that apply in concrete cases principles that the law faculty teach their students. Most medical school faculties include a high proportion of professors whose primary income is from their practice and whose allegiance to the medical school is sometimes loose.

The success of these ventures has depended heavily on moving the scholars to a different setting. The universities are not as adept at organizing their faculties to address real-world issues as the scholars are themselves when they move to government or another setting. The traditional cultural milieu of academe weighs heavily against such activities unless there is a strong counter-constituency to which the professors owe allegiance. Such is the case among some professional schools, particularly law and medicine and occasionally business, where the most successful graduates do not become professors, as is characteristic of the arts and sciences, but rather practitioners. These are also professions in the United States that are both more highly regarded and better remunerated than academe. But even these faculties have been beset by bitter internal disputes about the proper balance between theoretical and applied knowledge in the education of their students. Valuing the improvement of practice in any field comes hard in the university.

Certainly one of the most successful efforts at combining

research and application has been state university support of agriculture, initiated by the Morrill Acts of 1862 and 1890, the Hatch Act of 1887, and the Smith-Lever Act of 1914. In the case of that legislation, a politically powerful outside constituency, farmers, were not able to make a living from their crops and reluctantly turned to the universities for assistance. In the beginning they were not enthusiastic or optimistic that the universities could do anything to help them, and for a while they were correct. Legislators had more faith that the university could help than did either the farmers or the professors. Eventually, though, the universities, through their Schools of Agriculture and their Agricultural Experiment Stations, proved their ability to be genuinely helpful to farmers. An early example was the Babcock test for the butterfat content of milk, developed at the University of Wisconsin, which allowed farmers to analyze their cows' milk for the all-important level of cream and then to breed herds accordingly. Here was a triumph of some basic but mostly applied university research, driven by a powerful outside political constituency in the A & M institutions, which were dependent for their financing on state and federal funds. The clout of the constituency was greater than the academic culture, so much so that faculties in liberal arts departments at powerful A & M institutions heard themselves referred to as "service departments." The proper balance between theoretical and applied knowledge has been hard for universities to strike.

In the 1970s, when I was one of the academics recruited to serve in the government, a common refrain in Washington, D.C., was that universities should adapt their agricultural county agent/home demonstration agent model to serve schools as the agents have longed served farms. Several obstacles prevented that idea from coming to fruition: Albert Quie, its chief proponent, was not reelected from his Minnesota district to the House of Representatives; no consensus, outside of some circles of educators, had yet formed in the 1970s that American schools were in serious trouble and that their troubles had harmful consequences for American society; and neither universities nor their logical component for such a project, their schools of education, showed any interest in it. Today many Americans, educators and non-educators alike, believe that schools need improvement, that children need help. Sufficient changes may even be occurring within academe so that universities will come to support their schools of education in their efforts to improve schools and help children.

Strengthening Schools of Education

Structurally, schools of education are the most obvious point of contact between children's education and the university. I have so far avoided discussion of schools of education because I believe it is imperative that the university as a whole recognize the importance of improving the education of the young. Given the culture of universities, it is all too easy for faculty and administrators to view the pesky problems of poor, unhealthy, unmotivated, semiliterate teenagers as exclusively the concern of the school of education, which is often the weakest, poorest, and least prestigious faculty within the university. To view children's problems in this way is to assign children's fate to a faculty likely to be short of resources, both fiscal and intellectual. When the school of education turns out to be unable to solve the problems of children's health, development, and education, the university can interpret this as simply added evidence that the school of education is inadequate. But a university that takes this attitude is relinquishing its own role as an educational institution and ignoring its obligation to contribute to the education of the next generation.

Just as the missionless, impoverished, classics-oriented colleges of the mid-nineteenth century transformed themselves into universities, so may the universities of the late twentieth century discover contributions that they, not just their faculty on location elsewhere, can make to solving important problems afflicting the society. Schools of education are an excellent place to start.

Schools of education in the United States have had a turgid

history. Still widely admired abroad, where they are thought to be the best in the world, they have received little adulation at home. At least three times in this century my own institution, the Harvard Graduate School of Education, has faced the possibility of elimination by the Harvard Governing Boards. On one occasion in 1931 the university's president, A. Lawrence Lowell, advised the Harvard Board of Overseers that its school of education was "a kitten that ought to be drowned."[9] Similar fates have befallen schools of education in other major universities. During the past twenty-five years, three major private universities (Yale, Duke, and Chicago) have either eliminated or significantly reduced their faculties of education. In the mid-1980s, even Stanford considered such action, and the University of California at Berkeley came within a whisker of closing its school, while the University of Michigan cut resources in its school of education by almost 40 percent.[10]

Despite this institutional turbulence, or perhaps because of it, two unusual meetings occurred in the late summer and early fall of 1983. The first, at Pajarro Dunes, California, was called by Harvard president Derek Bok and Stanford president Donald Kennedy. They brought together the presidents of a small number of research universities (Columbia, Michigan, California, Wisconsin, Chicago) and some of the deans of their schools of education. The question before them was: What can we as institutions, and in particular our schools of education, do to improve public schools? Less than two months later another group, primarily deans of schools of education in research universities, convened at Wingspread in Racine, Wisconsin. This group, led by Judith Lanier, dean of the School of Education at Michigan State University, came together to discuss the question: How can we improve our schools of education, particularly our teacher education programs? The former meeting emphasized the university-wide responsibility for assisting public schools and the latter the unique responsibility of schools of education for preparing teachers.

What was most important about these meetings was that their

occurrence signified new concern about education: concern on the part of research university presidents about public education, a novelty in this century, and concern on the part of deans of schools of education at research universities about teacher education, also nearly a novelty in this century. In the twentieth century most presidents of research universities focused on developing their research missions, their international reputations, and their alumni support. And deans of schools of education, attempting to survive in universities emphasizing research, international reputations, and alumni support, not surprisingly gave the preparation of teachers for the American public schools a low priority as well. Hence, many major universities either dropped teacher education entirely or consigned it to academic oblivion. One dean who did not was Henry Holmes, dean of Harvard's school of education from 1920 to 1940. (Later, from 1973 to 1983, Harvard, too, eliminated most of its teacher education.)

Since the initial meeting at Wingspread, the deans of schools of education have formed the Holmes Group, named after Harvard's Holmes, and have reached out to include their university leaders in the efforts to reform teacher education. Progress is slow, but reform is now high on many institutional agendas, something that has not been true for many years.

But there is still more that schools of education can do to aid children and schools. Any professional school must be in a state of tension with its profession. That tension requires that the professional school be both knowledgeable and concerned about the profession's problems, and that those problems form the heart of the school's agenda. Such knowledge and concern imply that the professional school should be neither an uncritical supporter nor a carping critic of the profession.

A first vitally important way schools of education can help the schools is to improve the training of teachers. Schools of education, particularly in the finest research universities, have often kept their distance from their colleagues in the schools. One reason for the Holmes Group's decision to focus upon

teacher education was the admirable conviction on the part of
Judith Lanier and her colleagues that their schools of education
were not devoting enough of their resources—of both mind and
money—to teacher education, preferring higher-status pursuits
such as applied psychology or policy studies. It is time for a
sharper focus in schools of education on teachers, their initial
preparation, their continuing education, and their working conditions.

When schools of education do make efforts to reform teacher
training, they need the strong support of university leaders. This
is particularly important for academically selective colleges and
universities. Traditionally these institutions have not produced
many public school teachers. Harvard College, in fact, did not
have a teacher-training program for its undergraduates for its
first 348 years. Beginning teachers typically come from colleges
and universities that admit nearly everyone, particularly from
their own state, who applies. Many excellent teachers have come
from these institutions, but many other potentially fine teachers
have chosen undergraduate liberal arts programs in selective
colleges and universities, such as Rice, Amherst, Williams,
SUNY Binghamton, Oberlin, or Carleton.

Some of these students may go on to graduate work in education to become fully certified as teachers, but many may not
be willing to make such a counter-cultural (and expensive) choice
without trying teaching first to see if they like it. The institutions
they attend should provide options for them to get certification
so that such able people can be attracted to teaching. It is an
irony of the first order that a person completing a bachelor's
degree in education at XYZ State College can be certified to
teach in most states yet the baccalaureate in history from Stanford is required to study for an additional year before being
allowed to teach. Institutions need to support those able undergraduates who can manage to combine their liberal arts and
major requirements with an additional 15 or 18 credit hours in
education, including student teaching (less than 15 percent of
their undergraduate program), so that they can be certified upon

graduation. Our children would benefit from such lively, committed young teachers.

As state certification patterns change and teacher licensing evolves, many more options undoubtedly will come to exist for recruiting able persons to teaching. Wendy Kopp's Teach for America is one current effort. Kopp, who wrote her senior thesis at Princeton on the need to recruit able young people to teaching, has recruited recent liberal arts college graduates, provided summer training for them, and sent them to cities where they have been hired (and, owing to the fiscal plights of many urban areas, are now being laid off) as regular teachers.[11] Strong private schools where the academic ethos is powerful will probably continue to recruit new teachers without professional training, but public schools serving children without such strong familial and institutional supports for education will need teachers who not only know their subject but also know how to help hesitant students learn it. Giving them such knowledge is the role of schools or departments of education, and colleges and universities should support these schools and departments in that endeavor.

Second, schools of education can do much to improve the preparation of educational administrators, particularly ones for urban areas. Superintendents of urban schools invariably report a shortage of well-prepared educational leaders rising in the system. Few schools of education focus on the distinctive needs of urban systems and the special skills their administrators must have. In the city schools too many children and families face a whole panoply of difficulties, and school officials need to learn how to integrate their educational mission with efforts to meet the larger social needs of these children and their families. This is a daunting task, as any city school superintendent or principal will testify. Mobilizing unstable community support for this enterprise is of fundamental importance and requires political and media skills of a high degree. And above all a successful administrator must have a vision of what public schools can do—and what they cannot do—and the ability both to articulate and to

implement that vision. The individuals faced with these enormous expectations come to their jobs with little help from schools
of education, where all have studied, usually part time, while
fully employed as administrators of lower rank in the schools.

Similarly, at this time of unprecedented attention to the need
for "school site managers"—persons who assume greater responsibility at the school-building level—schools of education
need to provide preparation for this new type of administrator.
Either how to prepare beginning administrators for this novel
and as yet unrealized world or how to prepare experienced administrators for an altogether different world from the one they
have known is a taxing question indeed. Lessons from the business community, which has undergone some fundamental restructuring and concomitant retraining of its personnel, may be
particularly helpful here.

Administrative preparation provides an important opportunity for schools of education to collaborate not only with the
business community but with other parts of universities also
interested in the preparation of leaders and managers. Faculties
of public administration or public policy, faculties of public
health, as well as faculties of business, are natural allies of education schools in such preparation programs. Case materials for
instruction are much better developed for business, public policy, and public administration than they are for elementary and
secondary education, and while some educational problems are
distinctive, there are many areas of overlap. If integrated social
services are ever to be delivered at the school building or are
to be better coordinated in the community, then school administrators need to be in closer professional contact with those
responsible for the other services. Such colleagueship might well
start in graduate school in interdisciplinary seminars focusing on
delivering services (educational, legal, health, welfare) to children. Within the university classroom the friendships that facilitate subsequent professional networks could originate. This
cooperation among various faculties is unlikely to occur on most
university campuses unless university leaders specifically foster

it through positive incentives. For example, courses taught by several faculty members from different departments might be funded by the central administration rather than by the individual departments.

Full-time Graduate Study for Educators

To improve training for both teachers and administrators, schools of education need financial support so that a higher proportion of their students can study full time. Too much instruction in schools of education, especially at the graduate level, is provided one evening per week, either at the campus or at a distant site, to overworked and overtired school people who need the credit for certification or salary increments or both. Such settings are not conducive to serious learning or effective teaching, and much of the criticism of the inadequacies of education school courses is based on experience with models such as these.

No highly regarded professional programs in medicine or law are part time, and for good reason: the university cannot immerse the students in the culture of the profession unless they are present on a full-time basis. Students who are working full time at a job inevitably must give their major attention to that obligation, and the occasional university course in education cannot command their full attention. Few graduate schools of education enroll predominantly full-time students, largely because most cannot provide the financial aid that would be necessary to support such experienced practitioners. Hence, the model of the Harvard Business School with its intensive, focused two-year program to train general managers is not available to schools of education, and the preparation of school people suffers.

Since graduate study in education is almost always part time, it is fitted into the crevices of a life already overloaded with professional obligations that cannot all be fulfilled adequately. Under such circumstances professors limit their requirements, and the graduate student educators rarely visit the library, attend lectures by distinguished scholars or educators, or join informal discussions with other students and faculty about educational issues. Professional bonds are not formed through university study but rather with colleagues in the schools, thus vitiating significantly the influence of the university upon educators. No self-respecting professional school should let such a pattern develop in which its influence is inevitably minimized.

Schools of education must adapt their programs so that they can attract and support for full-time study able persons seeking to be practitioners: teachers, superintendents, and other types of administrators. Such programs will be expensive if they are done well and hence they will need financial help not only from the university but also from government, philanthropy, and business. The current lack of financial support for the education of all but a tiny fraction of our school administrators and teachers is an example of society's unwillingness to invest in the preparation of those who educate our young. It is, thus, another expression of America's ambivalence about the importance of education for everybody.

In the interim before full funding of all graduate students during the academic year can be achieved, a less expensive alternative that should be pursued is a series of residential summer programs in which university faculty and experienced practitioners can devote their full attention to the problems at hand, where library and other resources are available, and where the practitioners can benefit from prolonged discussions with one another and with university faculty away from their regular jobs. Such programs are routine for promising business executives, and companies support them because they believe that the corporation will benefit. Education should do the same.

Finally, leaders of schools of education and of universities need to continue their efforts to strike the proper balance in their faculties between issues of school improvement and broader educational issues. Both foci are vital for a first-class professional school. Today some schools of education concern themselves solely with preparation of school teachers and school administrators in their locale, while others concentrate entirely on other more expansive educational questions to the exclusion of schooling. Some are too narrow, and some are too broad. Finding and maintaining the proper balance between research and practice is the key.[12]

The difficulties schools of education have faced in their universities—low prestige and often low funds—mirror many of the problems that elementary and secondary schools face in American society. Like the schools they serve, schools of education are much better than they were in the early years of this century, but again like the schools, they have plenty of room for improvement. Faculties of schools of education are no longer largely populated by former school superintendents who regale their classes with the educational equivalent of war stories. Nor are there as many ex-teachers who bask in the greater professional respectability of university faculties and professional organizations. Most schools of education have not made smooth transitions from faculties of ex-schoolpeople to researchers who eschew the schools to professors who combine skill in research and in practice. Like their colleagues in the arts and sciences, most ed school professors today would rather explain a problem than solve it. Partly this is because the university culture in which they live and work places a higher value on explanation than on solution, and partly it is because the educational problems presented in America today are so daunting and are only partially rooted in issues of improved schooling and research.

The vineyard in which professors of education labor is one in which knowledge is important, but knowledge alone will not solve the educational problems of America. It can help, though, and faculties of education can make a limited but crucial contribution to improving the lot of American children and schools. Schools of education do not have it in their power to eliminate poverty, or to make American society place a higher value on its children or its schools. Graduate study in education should increase teachers' and administrators' understanding both of how children learn and of how institutions function, as well as improve their skills at enhancing both the learning and the functioning. These are no small accomplishments, and at a time when higher education's utility to society is being questioned, universities ignore them at their peril.

Graduate students in education at Clark University in Atlanta will not solve all the problems of the residents of the public housing project where they are working and living, just as even the most effective public school in Atlanta or any other city will not solve all the problems of the students there. Nonetheless, the task for schools of education and their universities is first to recognize the educational dilemmas faced by children and schools and then to work as best they can to resolve them. This is a goal neither recognized nor acted upon by most universities in the United States today.

· 5 ·

Business

Civic and business leaders in Kansas City are frustrated by the city's schools. They have worked hard to bring improvements to their schools, but they are not satisfied with the results. They recognize that some individual schools are educating children well, but many of the schools are not, despite what the leaders believe to have been significant efforts on their part to increase per pupil expenditures, to raise teachers' salaries, to improve curriculum materials, to enhance schools' use of technology, and various other efforts. When I was there recently, a new school superintendent had just been announced, and I did not hear anyone offer an encouraging word about the likelihood that he would be able to improve the schools.

Kansas City has been operating under a desegregation order for well over a decade, and this new superintendent is the eighth to serve in that time. Largely as a result of the court order, the business and civic leaders have agreed to greater investment in their schools, and they have even supported efforts to obtain a metropolitan school district that would be more heterogeneous racially and economically than the current district, but they have not seen immediate improvements in the academic achievement of the students. They are busy people, and some believe that, by now, positive changes should have occurred. As one civic leader told me, "We took the superintendent to breakfast for eight months and nothing happened."

The issues in Kansas City are familiar: mostly poor and mostly minority children are enrolled in schools that hire teachers and administrators who would like to be academically helpful to the children but who find that the circumstances of the children's lives and of the schools' routines impede them from being effective. Some teachers and administrators simply give up; many others remain willing to try but are unsure of what to do.

Some in the business community believe a single, dramatic solution to the problem must exist if only it can be found. "Governance," in this instance meaning a division of the existing district into three units, appeals to some. Others with a longer view of the situation understand that change will come slowly and will require political liaisons between the predominantly white, affluent, and socially prominent business leadership and the school board and educators. One very successful business-man reported that he had bought out all the local bookstores' stock of Lisbeth Schorr's *Within Our Reach*, in order to give copies to his friends so that they could understand both the problems children face and their solutions. Unlike many of his colleagues, he also maintained a cordial relationship with the head of the school board, who was not a business leader, and he hoped that doing so would help forge a link between the business community and the school leadership. Valuable as these efforts are, they satisfied no one, including him. Schools in nearby districts seem to function well—the schools of Independence, Missouri, have just become Medicaid vendors for the benefit of their pupils, and an elementary school in Johnson County, Kansas, has been selected as one of the most innovative schools in the nation because of a plan to deliver academic, social, and health services to its children—but the Kansas City ones do not. Frustration about schools is rampant in the city's business community. Businesspeople are dissatisfied with the academic performance of the students and graduates, and they find the administration of the schools inept.

The fundamental problems of the Kansas City schools will not be solved, in my view, by any single program initiated by the business community, such as mentoring, adopt-a-school, or any other currently popular plan. Nonetheless, it is important for community leaders to have some short-term, identifiable involvement with the schools, because few will engage in the long-term lobbying that is fundamentally necessary to change the circumstances of children unless they themselves have had some immediate and direct contact with the children and the schools. Thus, the strategy for involving businesses in school improvement must be one that includes short-term activities, such as building personal relationships with educators and children; medium-term ones, such as training teachers and administrators for restructuring of the schools; and long-term ones, such as vigorous political advocacy for children.

This is not a problem for Kansas City alone. American businesses share with families, government, and higher education the concern about American young people, and in recent years have come to understand that they, too, have both an obligation and a self-interest in aiding the young and in helping the schools to educate them more effectively. Business efforts to date have focused with particular urgency upon city schools because the headquarters of many leading businesses and the most acute examples of both impoverished youth and ineffective schools live in close proximity to each other in urban America.

American business, which depends on a supply of recent high school or college graduates to fill entry-level jobs, and which desires a strong economy in which to function, understandably shudders at dropout rates of 50 or 60 percent in nearby high schools, at graduates who are unsatisfactory employees, at soaring unemployment rates among young minority adult males. Jorie W. Philippi reports the following finding from a business survey: "Only one out of five high school graduates who apply for a position is functioning at a basic skills level acceptable for entry-level hiring, and of those hired, only one out of three is retained for longer than 90 days. Turnover rates for entry-level positions are often quoted as being as high as 150–300 percent."[1]

In the cities the problems are especially acute. In 1988 the New York Telephone Company tested 60,000 applicants to fill 3,000 entry-level jobs, according to Ronald K. Shelp, president of the New York City Partnership, a group formed to foster cooperation between education and business. While in the nation as a whole 55.3 percent of those aged sixteen to nineteen are either working or seeking full- or part-time employment, in New York City only 24.8 percent are, a statistic that undoubtedly reflects the startlingly high unemployment rates among poor teenagers of all ethnicities. The lack of a stream of qualified candidates for employment is part of the reason why many prominent firms either have left New York City or are considering doing so.[2]

Just as disturbing, the real median annual income for males in their twenties who are not college graduates is now considerably below what it was in 1959.[3] Meanwhile, the fraction of the workforce that is white and male is decreasing while the fractions that are female and minority are increasing: racial and ethnic minorities are expected to compose more than half of the growth in the U.S. workforce over the next decade. Since the academic performance of minorities still trails that of whites, and since girls' achievement in mathematics and science so far is lower than that of boys, these figures do not augur well for the new employees. For example, 47 percent of all blacks and 29 percent of all Hispanics aged twenty-one to twenty-five read below the eighth-grade level, compared to 15 percent of all whites.[4] Many scholars stress that grade-level indicators do not convey what we need to know about persons' knowledge and their ability to apply it in a work setting. Some draw a distinction between types of reading, calling the kind of reading taught in school "reading to remember" and reading at the workplace "reading to do."[5] Nonetheless, whatever one calls it, reading levels below the eighth grade do not suggest that those adults can either remember or do very well. Estimates vary on how much business spends on employee training, much of it remedial, but $45 billion annually is frequently cited. American business and its leaders are increasingly recognizing that these factors do not create a healthy environment for their companies, and that their future rests in part on improving the education of the young.[6]

Reluctance to Support Education

In the 1980s, as problems in both education and business became more apparent, business groups reluctantly began to address the issues of schooling. Initial efforts concentrated on telling the schools how badly they were educating the young and at what unnecessary expense. Representatives of the business community were quick to blame the problems of industry in international competition on the poorly prepared American workers. And yet at the same time some business groups led campaigns to reduce spending on education. In Massachusetts, for example, the High Tech Council led the lobbying for Proposition 2½, which was voted in in 1980 and which limited property taxes, the primary source of local funding for schools. A decade later, when high tech companies were suffering economically, the Council was again the principal lobbying group for another tax reduction plan that would have dramatically reduced funds for public education, the Citizens for Limited Taxation proposition, which was supported by the Republican candidate for governor, William Weld. Massachusetts voters elected Weld but defeated the tax reduction proposition.

In Mississippi the gas and oil industries lobbied successfully in 1982 to avoid an educational reform financed by severance taxes on their products, and the eventual reform was paid for by sales and income taxes. In the mid-1980s West Virginia attempted an educational reform to be paid for through increased property taxes, which was vigorously opposed by that state's most powerful industries, coal, timber, and minerals. Their opposition scuttled the reform.[7] In 1990, when Congress passed the Family and Medical Leave Act, which would have required companies with more than fifty employees to provide unpaid

leave of up to twelve weeks per year to care for new babies or
sick family members, a highly desirable arrangement for families,
some business organizations lobbied against it, and when President Bush vetoed it, John Motley, a vice president of the National Federation of Independent Business, exclaimed, "From
our standpoint it's a great day."[8] Some school boards, presumably concerned about a predominantly female teaching force,
also did not endorse the legislation.

Educators and businesspeople have great difficulty genuinely
communicating with each other. Their frames of reference and
their modes of tackling problems are very different. The clarity
of the principle of the bottom line does not exist for educators.
Mid-level school administrators sometimes have little understanding of meeting a budget, assuming that deficit financing
with public dollars will occur. Educators, unlike managers in
the private sector, do not have the option of discontinuing a
product line when it is unprofitable, difficult, or not wanted.
Extensive training and motivational incentives or reprisals for
managers and workers are common in the private sector, rare
in public schools. The organizational and management differences between schools and businesses are considerable, and
these actual differences but seeming similarities of administrative tasks impede genuine understanding of each other's enterprise.

School people are often either intimidated or irritated by
self-assured business leaders who come to them and tell them
how to organize themselves and how to run their institutions
more efficiently and competitively. Just how are we to do that,
they ask, in the face of all the demands and constraints we face
every day? Successful businesspeople, on the other hand, are
appalled at the bureaucratic rigidities and administrative slug-
gishness besetting schools. In a recent poll by *Fortune* magazine
of four hundred CEOs of large firms, more than three-quarters
of them rated public education as "fair" or "poor."[9]

When they get closer to the inner-city schools, many business
leaders are aghast at the manifold problems afflicting the children

who are enrolled. Two Milwaukee CEOs served as principals of local public schools one winter day and returned to a board dinner in the cozy Milwaukee Club and poignantly reported the day's primary dilemma: what to do with a homeless adolescent in fifteen-degree weather? Under such circumstances improving computational skills is a less immediate need than providing a warm, safe place for supper and sleep.

Sometimes veterans of the private sector seek remedies, such as private schools for the poor, that allow the application of their customary principles of competition and motivation. Often called "vouchers" or variations on "choice" plans, such efforts typically provide funds for a child to attend a private school of the family's selection. Sometimes all the options are within the public schools, but the most fervent advocates usually prefer schools that are independent of the regulatory requirements of public funding. They point with legitimate pride to the successes of a number of Roman Catholic schools in educating poor city children.

There is no question that some of these schools provide a fine education for their students. The policy dilemma, however, is how to gain the benefits of these programs for all children. The non-public schools are free to dismiss children if they choose (drop the product line, so to speak), but the dismissed children still need an education, probably more acutely than do the children remaining in the school. Private schools also have a modicum of parental support, since families have gone to the trouble of seeking this educational alternative for their children. These schools can also run more cheaply, since they can be selective about which children they choose to admit, avoiding, for example, educable mentally retarded, emotionally disturbed, or profoundly physically handicapped children. Furthermore, without the burden of reporting on the use of public funds a school needs fewer administrators.

Business leaders are divided on the wisdom of these alternatives, as are educators. The powerful report on education issued in the spring of 1991 by the Committee for Economic

Development, *The Unfinished Agenda: A New Vision for Child
Development and Education,* supported policies allowing families to select schools within the public system only, but three
members of its fifty-seven-member research and policy committee disagreed. "To limit choice plans to the public schools
would significantly undercut the effectiveness of choice as a tool
for educational reform," one dissenter argued. The remainder
of the committee supported limiting choice to the public
schools.[10]

Nor do business leaders and educational administrators di-
agnose the problems in the same ways. Administrators generally
believe the major factors contributing to poor student achievement are changes in family structure, low student and teacher
motivation, and cuts in state and local budgets, while business
leaders typically cite a lack of emphasis on teaching basic skills,
undermotivated or poorly trained teachers, and low academic
standards.[11] Undoubtedly teachers, if asked, would also mention
unresponsive administrators. The cultures of business and
schools remain very different, and neither is well understood
by the other. The cultural chasm between them impedes their
communication and hence their cooperation. Frequently the
chasm is now bridged by politesse, preferable to the former
mode of carping criticism certainly, but not an effective means
of bringing disparate groups to candor about their common problems and hence to solutions of them.

The uncertainty of the last quarter of the twentieth century
has led American business, however reluctantly, to pay greater
attention to education, of both its current and its future workers.
The initial educational efforts by firms concentrated on their
own employees, a long-standing tradition in well-managed companies. During the 1980s many large businesses were rapidly
and dramatically expanding their in-house education or training
programs to encompass broader and increasingly remedial skills.
Understandably, companies facing increasing foreign competition were not eager to spend their own money training employees in skills they believed formal schooling should have

provided. This is one explanation for the repeated criticism by business leaders of the poor performance on standardized tests of American youth in comparison with youngsters in other industrialized nations.

In the 1980s those in the experienced workforce without adequate skills, particularly the ability to learn new techniques of work and management, were facing layoffs and early retirement. Management continued to invest significantly in the preparation of its potential senior managers, both through in-house programs and by supporting them to attend conferences and multi-week seminars. Some companies, such as Motorola, which remained American-owned and still competitive internationally, were making enormous educational investments in their own employees.[12]

By the late 1980s, faced with declining productivity, business was focusing not only on in-house education but on the inadequate skills of entry-level workers, thereby bringing the interests of companies and schools closer together. Some American managers had a tendency to blame falling productivity on the educational inadequacies of the employees rather than on factors inherent in the operations of the company itself. In fact, both these factors are important, as Richard J. Murnane points out in commenting upon the GM-Toyota NUMMI automobile project, in which an old workforce with new management techniques transformed itself from inefficient to efficient.[13]

Better schools, by themselves, will not solve the problems of American business, as all thoughtful and perceptive businessmen recognize. Nonetheless, a better-educated workforce would be an asset to business, giving it more flexibility in how workers are used in a company and thus allowing for different forms of organization, and also requiring fewer resources to be devoted to compensating for workers' deficiencies. At this time in our history it is critical because, as Murnane has observed, "education is particularly important in fostering productivity growth when production processes are changing and new technologies are being introduced."[14] Thus, the question is: What are the most appropriate steps for American business to take to accomplish the laudable objective of improving the education of Americans?

Old Links with Schools

Traditionally American business leaders, most of them men, have had two major links with the schools: membership on school boards in their local communities, and participation in their children's schools. In recent years school board membership for such executives has substantially declined, particularly in cities, and for many the parental role of school involvement is a decade or two past. Certainly neither of these experiences effectively prepares today's leaders for the reality of the urban schools and their manifold problems. Occasionally a leader's daughter, rarely a son, may be employed for a time as a teacher, thus giving her father an additional insight into the world of schooling. In the male-dominated world of CEOs, schooling is women's work.

A great loss to city schools brought about by the suburbanization of America since World War II has been the loss of these business families—first of their children, who brought with them high expectations for the schools, and secondly of the business leaders themselves, who no longer participate directly in the governance of the schools. In particular, the absence of business leaders from city school boards is an immense loss; their organizational and budgetary expertise would be very helpful in those complicated settings. Although the influence of powerful men on school boards was much decried by George S. Counts in 1927,[15] today it is a rare city in which the leadership of the school board involves many powerful leaders of the entire community. More typical are representatives of particular groups, often identified by ethnicity or religion, who are expected to forge coalitions to benefit both their constituencies and the community as a whole. Many have difficulty doing so. Often service on the school board is their major position of responsibility, and given their limited organizational experience, they have little appreciation of the distinction between policy and administration, often preferring administration—and the opportunities for intervention and sometimes graft it presents—to policy. The corruption of the community school board and the harassment of the superintendent revealed in 1989–90 in Queens, New York, exemplify the problem.

Most school boards are not corrupt, although political pressures for appointment of staff and awarding of service contracts are common. Many boards, because of the lack of experience of their members, get bogged down in drawn-out decision making procedures that are the opposite of good business practice. In many cities, for example, boards meet biweekly or even more often for several hours at a time, something no well-organized executive would put up with. The vicissitudes of dealing with such boards have led to the premature resignation of many able superintendents. The Boston School Committee spent much of the winter of 1989–90 deciding whether to fire Superintendent Laval Wilson and buy out the remainder of his contract, and after finally deciding to do so, named an interim superintendent in March. One year later the board was still thinking about possible candidates to succeed Wilson. The new superintendent, Lois Harrison Jones, who began work in July of 1991 without a contract, was to be Boston's eighth in eleven years.

In one major city the chair of the school board, a smart, tough, and honest woman, is an employee of the local telephone company, and her supervisor has recently allowed her to take considerable time off from her job in order to devote herself to city school activities. While that is a laudable decision for her and the telephone company, it also reflects the absence from the leadership of the board of persons with broad recognition and power in the community. School boards need the community representation they have recently been getting, but they also need the experience and clout that business leaders could give.

In New York City such an individual, Richard I. Beattie, a white male resident of Manhattan and a senior partner in a major law firm, was removed by Mayor Koch so that Koch could replace him with a Hispanic from the Bronx. Beattie supported a greater voice for Hispanics in the New York schools, but his service to the city in this manner was abruptly terminated. His experience may have dissuaded some like-minded colleagues from wishing to get involved in such politically fractious activities. Schools and children lose when experienced, committed, able people do not serve.

A further disadvantage of the absence of successful business-people from school boards is that such boards are unlikely to be able to reach and influence the city's nonresident business leaders who are concerned about the problems of the city's schools, and who might be persuaded to participate in the search for solutions. If the schools are to be run more efficiently and more effectively, and if they are to form mutually beneficial relationships with the business community, then business leaders need to play more direct roles in the governance of the city schools. Under present circumstances few are likely to be willing or able to do so, just as a massive return of middle- and upper-class children to the city public schools is unlikely. Therefore, those two traditional ties of business leadership with the public schools—through school board membership and parenthood—while still desirable, cannot be the primary focus of business involvement with schools for the future. Other links must be forged.

New Links with Education

One of those potentially powerful new links is the set of business groups that began organizing themselves in the 1980s to attend to issues of children and their education. Spearheaded by several of its own organizations, including the Committee for Economic Development (CED), the Business Roundtable, the National Alliance of Business, and now the Chamber of Commerce, American business rediscovered the schools during the 1980s, and many business leaders are provocatively and imaginatively pondering what they can do to help them. Owen B. Butler, retired chairman of Procter & Gamble and current chair of the CED, has been indefatigable as a spokesman for the business community and its concern for educational improvement, thus following in the tradition of one of his predecessors at Procter & Gamble, Neil McElroy, who led business efforts for education in the 1950s. David Kearns, the former chairman of Xerox, has written with Denis P. Doyle a well-received book on the subject, *Winning the Brain Race.*[16] Other current CEOs have spoken widely about education and testified in Congress in support of education legislation, for Chapter I in 1987 (when more than one hundred CEOs were asked in order to get four to testify), for Head Start in 1989, and for WIC (Special Supplemental Food Program for Women, Infants and Children) in 1991. Apparently it was not difficult to recruit James Renier of Honeywell, Robert Winters of Prudential Insurance, Robert Allen of AT&T, John Clendenin of BellSouth, and William Woodside of Sky Chefs, to make the case for full funding of WIC, which they observed would cost the equivalent of what was spent on three days of the Gulf War.

The Business Roundtable has agreed to pair the CEO of a major corporation with a governor in each state to work on ten-year plans for reform and restructuring of education aimed at achieving systemic change.[17] No longer are elementary and secondary education relegated solely to the corporate office dealing with community relations or public outreach. Today there is evidence that senior management is taking the education of the young seriously. For many managers this interest is stimulated by concern for their own businesses and for the general business climate in the United States, and by uncertainty about the role of education of the workforce in contributing to both. The key terms are "productivity" and "competitiveness" and the question is what education can contribute to each. It is striking that these business leaders who are focusing their attention upon education are not primarily interested in their own or their children's education, traditionally the only educational issues with which

laypersons have dealt, but in the education of someone else's
children. Those children, the business leaders hope, with the
right kind of education will grow up to be successful employees
and prosperous consumers.

A recent report by the MIT Commission on Industrial Productivity, *Made in America: Regaining the Productive Edge,*
deals in considerable detail with the patterns of outlook and
behavior besetting the American industries that have had difficulties. But the commission's conclusion focuses on education:

> The task of upgrading the primary and secondary schools is
> probably the single most important challenge facing the coun-
> try. We join with others in calling for federal support of local
> programs that are intended to strengthen primary and second-
> ary education. Commission members are acutely aware that
> the problems of public education in this country go well beyond
> the classroom to basic social and economic conditions . . .
> Merely increasing standards or the time in school will not suf-
> fice, however; ways must be found to better motivate students
> who do not currently see a good reason for staying in school.[18]

For most of us, motivation grows out of realistic hope. We
are motivated when we believe that genuine opportunities and
benefits will come to us if we follow a particular, possibly difficult, course. Lack of motivation among the young, particularly
those living in poverty in the inner city, is a reasonable attitude
for them, alas, and the task that we all face is giving them realistic
hope. Children who have rarely, if ever, seen someone they
know succeed in a legitimate endeavor through education and
hard work have difficulty believing that they themselves can do
so. Similarly, the man who cannot support his wife and child
above the poverty level while working full time at the minimum
wage has reason to feel discouraged, as do the men who are not
college graduates and whose incomes have steadily declined over
the last several decades. The MIT Commission is simply the

most recent of many thoughtful statements by business leaders and others who call for both school reform and social reform as being in the best interest of business.

Issues of reform are not new to American business. Many businesses have instituted significant reform in their own firms during the past decade, and others are undergoing such changes now. Still others are pondering their best strategies of satisfying their stockholders while avoiding unfriendly takeovers. In such a turbulent time for American companies, many leaders understandably do not want to hear that they must also assume positions of responsibility in educational reform. And even those who do wish to participate in improving the schools may not wish to hear that the reform of schools, interlaced as it is with society's dilemmas, is a long-term activity that cannot be measured in quarterly reports. The fundamental changes that need to come in American schools for the benefit of all of us are not likely to be seen by any sitting CEO during his tenure as his company's leader. William Woodside commented at a 1988 CED Symposium,

> I think most of us suffer from the seven-year itch: after the initial excitement and the publicity there comes a point when interest lags. You get tired, a little bored, and you don't hear the praise you once did. Motivation starts to go and inertia sets in. I am beginning to see these warning signals throughout the business community. We are, I think, very much focused in general on maybe not short-term results but short-term appreciable improvement. That is one thing that we are not going to see in the education field for a considerable time.[19]

Beset as many business leaders are by other problems, a number have nonetheless involved themselves in educational reform, recognizing that improving education is in the best interest of their own companies, of the U.S. economy, and of democracy in general. At the national level and in their many communities they have been discussing both what needs to be done to help children develop and learn and what business can do to assist in this effort. As the Kansas City example revealed, the strategy must be one that addresses fundamental problems, and inevitably that must be long-term. In the meantime there are some middle-range activities to support. And, there must be some short-term actions that will involve business and promise some immediate, if not long-lasting, successes. Thus, American business can make vital contributions to the education of America's children in three principal areas: advocating and fostering children's healthy development, supporting the restructuring of schools, and collaborating with individual schools or school systems.

Advocacy for Children

The greatest single contribution that business can make to the improvement of education in the United States is powerful advocacy for children. Our country works on the principle of advocacy. Groups push for what they want or need, and the pressure—political, economic, social, or moral—makes change more likely to occur.

Children in America need advocates and do not have them now. Business can supply advocacy for children, for their healthy development, and for their education. Advocacy means keeping children's issues on the public agenda and working with various groups, both public and private, to improve the circumstances of children's lives. Business understands advocacy; it engages in advocacy in its own behalf regularly. It needs to extend its definition of "its own behalf" to include the children who will become the employees it will hire and the consumers who will buy its products.

For children to learn, their health and development must be nurtured. That simple truism has been ignored by many of the recent school reform enthusiasts, but it is the starting point for any effort to increase the academic achievement of America's young. Those who are hungry or in poor health, physically or mentally, will have a much more difficult time mastering reading or mathematics than those who are fed and well.

Families, not government, nor schools, nor business, have the primary obligation to provide for children's well-being, but as we have seen in Chapter 2, not all families in the United States fulfill that obligation, either because of poverty, disintegration, selfishness, or some combination of all three. When families are unable or unwilling to give their children proper care, then some other supports must be provided for the children, who after all cannot care for themselves. This help is needed for the nation, not just the children, to flourish.

American business has come to understand international comparisons. The finding that U.S. infant mortality rates are higher than those of Japan, Sweden, Canada, Norway, France, Germany, Austria, the United Kingdom, and Italy suggests that all is not well in the health care that expectant mothers and newborns receive here. In a recent study on children's well-being undertaken by the U.S. Congress, about the only categories in which the United States led the world were the consumption of calories, not necessarily a standard of good health, and the divorce rate (64 percent higher than any other country studied), also not likely to be beneficial to children.[20]

Through blue ribbon commissions and through the testimony of its leaders on these matters, American business is helping to keep children's healthy development on the public agenda. The three reports by the Research and Policy Committee of the CED, *Investing in Our Children* (1985), *Children in Need* (1987), and *The Unfinished Agenda* (1991), are excellent, thoughtful commentaries on the long-term needs of our young. All recognize that the schools' "problems" are, in fact, embedded in the deeper difficulties of the society. None promises a quick fix or a magic-bullet solution to the educational dilemmas of America's children. These three documents represent American business at its strategic best, identifying fundamental issues and avoiding flashy but partial solutions.[21]

These impressive efforts by the CED illustrate the capacity

of American business leaders to identify a problem. The next
step is for them to use their genuine political muscle to move
public opinion and the legislative and executive branches of
government to do something about it. Several of the issues identified by the CED are ones that could be addressed through
additional public programs of daycare, health care, or education.
American business traditionally has demonstrated an ability to
convince Americans that they want or need a product. That same
expertise could do much if brought to bear on these children's
issues.

Thus far, the analysis is stronger than the implementation.
American business leaders can be quite adept at shaping tax
policy so that it will have an advantageous effect on their niche
in the industry. That same skill needs to be directed toward the
congressional and Cabinet staff who draft legislation that will
affect children. The testimony of CEOs is powerful, but the
quiet work of companies' congressional liaison staff is also necessary on these issues. Most federal lawmakers and regulators
are accustomed to dealing with lobbyists representing various
educational and public interest groups. Heretofore, the formidable teams developed by most companies to influence legislation
or regulations have not dealt with questions of health and human
services or education. A shift in their assignments to include
health and education issues as well as tax or tariff ones would
signal American business's concern with children and education
in a powerful and tangible fashion. Certainly business opposition
to the Family and Medical Leave Act was an important influence
leading to President Bush's veto of it. Powerful lobbying to
extend support for Head Start, Chapter I, and immunization to
cover all eligible children, for example, could have tremendous
benefits. So could support for child care legislation that would
make America competitive with France or Italy in the support
we give our children.

One of the great strengths of American business is its ability
to use the media to advance its interests and to shape public
opinion. If American business comes to believe broadly that

healthier and better-educated children are in its interests, then it may focus its media efforts on those issues. Obviously not all American businesses have exactly the same interest in the young. While Hewlett-Packard may be most concerned about developing mathematics skills in young people that will make them effective employees or affluent consumers, other companies may have lower expectations for them as either employees or consumers, as in the case of the New Hampshire high school student working at a fast food restaurant. Hence, to expect American business to speak with a single voice about its aspirations for the young is unrealistic. Nonetheless, insofar as a prosperous society, with qualified employees and well-off consumers, benefits business, business has a strong incentive to keep public opinion focused upon enhancing children's healthy development.

Currently much media attention is focused upon young people, urging them to buy food, much of which is not good for them, or clothes, with an emphasis on rapidly changing styles, or toys, which they often do not need. None of these efforts is consistent with encouraging either children's healthy development or their education. Public service announcements state the need to stay in school but generally convey this message without the attention-getting glitz associated with sugary cereals, designer jeans, or electronic games. If American business believes that the young do not have adequate academic skills or work habits, then companies need to restrict their own efforts to convince the young to consume goods that are often antithetical to healthy development and good education. Undoubtedly business would prefer self-policing in this regard to government regulation, but some indication from business that it is willing to undertake such a policing effort is vital.

In short, filling the need of businesses for better entry-level workers requires more than intervention at the high school level. If we truly want a healthy, industrious, capable, and committed workforce, then the values of our society, including those of American business, must be communicated forcefully to the young. Currently the message is decidedly mixed. If we are to expect stronger academic achievement, then business cannot cajole young people to spend their time and money on unhealthful and non-educational products and activities. Such contradictory efforts will not enhance children's education or give credibility to business's commitment to improving children's lives and education.

Helping Schools Restructure

While it is vital to get the children to school in the mood to learn, it is also essential that the schools be places in which learning is expected, valued, and likely to occur. Such is not the case in many American schools today. Ask teenagers what they think of school, and the common reply is "Boring." The central argument of Arthur Powell, Eleanor Farrar, and David Cohen's impressive book *The Shopping Mall High School* is that school people and students have made a private pact that neither will ask too much of the other, and that as long as the pact is neither made explicit nor challenged, the accommodation makes life easier for both students and faculty.[22] It does not, however, make life easier for the students when they seek employment or for employers who must train their new employees.

To change the schools into places that truly foster learning, major restructuring of educational institutions serving children will be required. Tinkering with individual school programs, valuable as that may be in particular cases, is not enough; systemic change, as the Business Roundtable effort promises, is required. Some of our finest American companies have had considerable experience recently in restructuring themselves effectively. That was Kearns's great achievement at Xerox. The schools also need effective restructuring, and the lessons and support of business would be particularly helpful in this endeavor.

As I have said, American public schools are different from American business in some extremely important ways: the schools function under very different incentive mechanisms;

they must serve all comers; they can not discard a product line when they no longer find it profitable or convenient. Historically educators have been severely criticized for indiscriminate adaptations of business practices to schools. The most influential of these were Frederick Winslow Taylor's time and motion studies, which were taken up by the school efficiency movement led by David Snedden in a previous era of school reform early in the twentieth century.[23] Present movements for reform in business are much less mechanistic than the advocacy of time and motion studies; rather, current discussion of business restructuring stresses the need to keep several factors simultaneously in mind (customers, suppliers, inventory, quality control, service), rather than rely on a single, all-purpose change in practice.

Any argument resting on interrelationships is more complicated than one focused on one factor, and generally requires a longer time for the achievement of its objective. Complexity and longevity certainly characterize the difficulties associated with restructuring the schools. As Richard F. Elmore and Milbrey Wallin McLaughlin entitled their Rand report, educational reform is *Steady Work*.[24] Restructuring the schools will provide no single, quick fix to the problem of children's education in America, but it is an important element in the broader strategy of enhancing children's lives and opportunities, and hence our national future.

One important lesson from current business reform is that it is comprehensive. It does not limit itself to a single plant or to one component of the company's production. Innovation may begin in a single site, but the goal is to transform the entire enterprise. So it must be with educational reform; change may start in a single building or even a single system, but it must become much wider to include not only the school but the broader educational influences upon the child, such as the family, the community, and television. So must it ultimately include the factors affecting the child's health and development. A focus upon the school is an appropriate beginning for the larger educational reform that is necessary. That reform must be structural and systemic, not resting on the skills of a single extraordinary teacher, principal, or superintendent. Particular schools or even systems are often too dependent upon key persons, charismatic teachers or administrators, for their success, and a system that enrolls nearly 40 million children and engages 2.5 million teachers cannot rely on the occasional outstanding individual for all its successes.

In addition to being complex, continuous, and comprehensive, school restructuring must also be collaborative. School people have considerable expertise themselves, and any restructuring effort must rest on that substantial and valuable base. Too often their wisdom has been ignored or discounted, both because it is theirs—and they are supposed to be part of the problem, not part of the solution—and because it is not codified. The potential contribution to school improvement of both teachers and administrators is enormous, as is their capacity to thwart the efforts of others to "fix" them. Thus, any group—community, government, higher education, or business—that seeks to restructure the schools must develop genuine alliances with those who work in the schools.

American business, at its best and fresh from its own restructuring efforts, understands that educational reform must be complicated, continuous, comprehensive, and collaborative. It must also be funded, and that is another concept that American business recognizes. Heretofore, educational philanthropy by American business has been concentrated in higher education, from which it has seen a more direct benefit, largely in supporting the advanced education of its employees or in research related to its product lines. Hence, chemical companies have aided chemistry and chemical engineering departments, insurance companies have contributed to economics departments and actuarial programs, and everybody has supported the best business schools.

Recently American business has concluded that a somewhat longer view of its best interest would include philanthropy in support of school reform. RJR Nabisco's Next Century Schools is an example of such an effort at school reform, which its CEO, Louis V. Gertsner, Jr., urges be radical. In 1990 in its initial grants the RJR Nabisco Foundation awarded $8.5 million to fifteen schools, which were chosen on the basis of their innovative educational programs. The winning schools are ones that are making dramatic changes in their programs and conceptions of schooling. Even innovations like these, however, are individual, school-based programs rather than steps toward systemic change. Citicorp has committed $20 million over the next ten years to the Coalition of Essential Schools, a dynamic effort to bring groups of schools to a common educational philosophy based upon fundamental learning for all children and to implement that philosophy.[25]

The more fundamental restructuring, which includes renewing and revitalizing the persons who work in schools, has not yet attracted significant portions of the business community's philanthropy. Ultimately, however, the greatest leverage for American business to improve the schools, and hence children's education, lies in restructuring, not in individual school projects.

The MIT Commission on Industrial Productivity, which cited the problems of American business, also discussed the strengths of those businesses which were successfully coping in the new economic environment. They found six similarities among those they termed the "best practice firms": (1) a focus on simultaneous improvement in cost, quality, and delivery; (2) closer links to customers; (3) closer relationships with suppliers; (4) the effective use of technology for strategic advantage; (5) less hierarchical and less compartmentalized organizations for greater flexibility; and (6) human-resource policies that promote continuous learning, teamwork, participation, and flexibility.[26]

To be concrete, let us look now at what those "best practice" characteristics might mean if adapted for the restructuring of schools:

Focus on simultaneous improvement in cost, quality, and delivery. Restructuring the schools requires changing the culture of the institutions so that these three factors are integrated in the minds of teachers and administrators. Heretofore they have not been, with administrators dispensing the funds but not controlling their origin. The school tax or millage remains for most Americans the only tax on which they can vote, and they do, often negatively when they do not have children in school, as most now do not. Today only 27 percent of U.S. households are couples with children, while the comparable figure for Japan, for example, is 39 percent.[27] Furthermore, the United States has a culture in which concern about children is seen as a family matter, not one for the society as a whole, and therefore the effect of the decline in the percentage of households with children is particularly stark here.

From its experience in restructuring, business could help change the internal culture of the school so that these three factors could be seen as interrelated and could help muster public support for more funds when needed, and could guide the careful management of the available funds. Such help could take the form, for example, of having businesspeople who have led effective restructuring of their companies spend significant periods of time (weeks or months) working full time in schools with teachers, administrators, and community leaders, building support for such changes. These efforts could be augmented by seminars for the educators with other businesspeople who would explain the elements of their companies' restructuring.

Closer links to customers. Public schools have simply assumed that children would attend them except for those who chose religious-sponsored schools or the tiny minority in most communities who chose independent schools. More than eighty-five percent of American children still attend public schools, but many public schools are realizing that they have an obligation to *attract* students, not simply to enroll them. Many magnet schools are based on this assumption. Most magnet schools have a specialty, such as mathematics and science, the arts, or foreign languages. Typically one has to apply in order to be admitted;

their principles of selection vary, often modified by desegregation plans that require that such schools not become havens
for one racial or ethnic group. The old examples of magnet
schools are Boston Latin, Bronx High School of Science, and
Brooklyn Tech. Now such schools are common in most cities, a
rejection of the principle that James B. Conant enunciated in
the 1950s of the superiority of the comprehensive high school.

The crucial issue, though, is that the non-magnet schools
must also serve their constituencies well. In short, the wishes
and interests of attending students and of their families are vital,
as discussed in Chapter 2. If the schools are to gain wider support
in society, a starting point is to gain the support of their own
"customers." Since attendance is mandatory, public schools
sometimes forget that their clientele must be wooed. Business
can help remind them. American businesses, from car makers
to toothpaste producers, have learned that they cannot take their
customers for granted but rather must consider their views.

Closer relationships with suppliers. The suppliers for the
schools are the families of the children. Frequently schools have
functioned without much thought to the impact of their policies
on family life, as we have seen in Chapter 2. For example, when
more than two-thirds of school-age children have working mothers, the schools still organize themselves on the assumption that
mother is waiting at home with milk and cookies at 3:00 P.M.
daily and is available full time during holiday and summer re-
cesses. School people, in collaboration with other providers of
service to children and families, need to create in their buildings,
if not in their academic programs, more varied kinds of care for
children. This may mean buildings that are open all day, all year,
with many services provided. Again, both expertise from business in devising new modes of integrating services and financial
support from business to establish them would be helpful. "Just
in time" modes of inventory, which coordinate delivery of supplies at the time when they are needed, thus avoiding large
warehousing costs, were brand-new to business a decade ago,

and some American companies have now mastered them. Surely some of those lessons of providing supplies are applicable to the provision of services.

Effective use of technology for strategic advantage. For teachers who may not even have a desk to call their own, the opportunity to have a PC would be remarkable. Most of the emphasis on technology in the schools has focused upon uses either by the student or by the administration. Much remains to be done in improving instructional uses of computer technology, particularly in providing good software. As business knows, good software is expensive to create, and funds have not been available for the development of excellent software devoted to teaching. Too often instructional software now resembles an electronic workbook, not a strategically sound use of technology. Teachers' uses of computers could also be dramatically expanded. For example, a project at the Harvard Graduate School of Education has created a computer network for first-year teachers: teachers can sit down at their PCs and type in questions or other messages for their fellow first-year teachers or for their graduate school faculty, and answers come back through the computer network. Early results show this system to have immense promise for helping beginning teachers in their critical first year. Business could help here with providing the software expertise, the equipment, and the knowledge of how computer networks function best.

Less hierarchical and less compartmentalized organizations for greater flexibility. Many public school systems remain in a rigid, bureaucratic vise. Nearly all administrators were formerly teachers, and yet the gap separating the two groups is immense. The administrative cadre grows while the number of teachers remains static or shrinks. The school reform literature calls for less "top down" management, but few teachers notice that change has occurred. Although "school site management" is touted as the panacea of school reform, little systemic change has occurred to make such management change happen. Both by providing its own examples of how "best practice firms" have changed their organizations and by funding teachers and administrators to learn new modes of management, business could aid the schools on this already recognized vital issue. Business has long understood that intensive training for employees and managers is essential if attitudes and behavior are to change. For public schools to move from their current managerial mode to one consistent with the new rhetoric, substantial changes must take place in the minds, hearts, and actions of both teachers and administrators. That is unlikely to occur unless significant investments are made in their education or training, but so far little has been provided beyond pronunciamentos and their functional equivalent, one-day workshops. If cultures are to change, investment in people is needed, and business both understands and can support such efforts.

Human-resource policies that promote continuous learning, teamwork, participation, and flexibility. If organizations are to be less hierarchical and less compartmentalized, then they must support and sustain the people who work in them. IBM estimates that it annually spends approximately $2 billion on the education of its 380,000 employees. Teachers, meanwhile, have a couple of "in-service" days annually at the system's expense. Most school systems have cut their sabbatical programs for teachers and administrators under the budget stringencies of recent years. Few pay for attendance at summer workshops even for topics, such as school site management, that are supposed to be of high priority for the district. As discussed in Chapter 4, few teachers or administrators have ever had a period of full-time study in their fields after becoming educators. Business support for graduate study for educators would be an excellent investment.

If business leaders believe continuing education is vital for their top people, then surely they must recognize that it is also vital for educational leaders. When opportunities do exist for educators to get additional study, typically it is on an individual basis, rarely for a group or team of teachers and administrators who wish to implement a new program. Support for that kind of work would be most valuable as well. Business, both by example and by funding, can help districts to recognize the value of such investment in their personnel.

As the projected teacher shortage approaches, one important way for businesses and schools to work together is in the preparation of early retirees to become teachers. At the Harvard Graduate School of Education we created the Mid-Career Math and Science Program, which began in 1983; over 85 percent of the graduates of this program have subsequently taught mathematics or the sciences, both subjects in which the shortage of qualified teachers is acute, and 68 percent of the program's graduates are still teaching. These individuals, who have successfully completed careers in the military, insurance agencies, electronics firms, chemical companies, the weather bureau, and a host of other scientific or technical fields, often make marvelous teachers, given both their commitment to teaching the young and their prior experience in utilizing mathematics and science. Many find the year of preparation at Harvard and in the schools financially difficult, and some companies have aided them by allowing them to work half-time their last two years with the company so they can complete the one-year program on a part-time basis; other companies have simply paid the tuition and a stipend for the retiree as part of a severance package. Many variations are possible, but potentially this is a very fruitful source of capable, committed, and nontraditional teachers.

"Restructuring" is the code word today in American schools. It has various immensely different meanings, but most often it is used to evoke whatever changes the speaker believes the schools need. Every reform movement needs a term under which diverse groups can form a coalition before they have agreed on the specifics of their agenda of change. "Restructuring" is such a term in the United States today, much as *perestroika* was in the Soviet Union in the mid-1980s. Let us hope that America's pursuit of the restructuring of its schools will be more successful and less traumatic than Gorbachev's efforts for his nation. Most proponents of restructuring believe in greater clarity of academic purpose and accountability for academic achievement for the school system; greater authority and responsibility at the school-building level for teachers, students, and administrators; and broader provision of services—academic, health, legal, welfare, and other—through the school system. How to accomplish all this remains the mystery.

Collaborating with Schools

The primary way in which business has involved itself to date with elementary or secondary education has been through collaboration with specific schools or school systems. These collaborations have been valuable in helping business learn about the realities of children's and educators' lives, but they have not produced basic improvements in the education of the young. They have, however, given businesspeople direct experience with schools, and in that regard have been useful in providing a short-term strategy for business involvement with education.

Such programs as the Boston Compact and the Boston Plan for Excellence, begun in 1982, are examples of business groups working together either to provide jobs for graduates of local high schools or to provide money for school-initiated projects that would improve the students' educations. In the former instance businesses simply said they would hire graduates of the Boston Public Schools in entry-level jobs, and in the latter, business provided funds for school improvement projects devised by teachers or administrators. These programs did no harm, but neither did they solve the problems of the Boston Public Schools. In the spring of 1991 Philadelphia, which has had a much closer relationship between school and business leaders and more stable school leadership (Superintendent Constance Clayton has served since 1982) than Boston, announced a five-year educational partnership between corporations and the public schools. In addition to promising job possibilities for high school graduates in Philadelphia, the busi-

ness community is also committed to financially supporting curriculum development and teacher and administrative training
programs, as well as lobbying the state for additional funds for
low-income students, all-day kindergarten, and special education programs. Meanwhile, the school district promises to raise
test scores and graduation and promotion rates by the mid-1990s.
This plan is more comprehensive and more long term than the
Boston efforts; it is based on much deeper understanding of the
educational problems that city schools face; and it is characterized by greater respect between business and educational leaders
than has been the case in many other cooperative efforts between
business and schools in urban areas.[28]

Many businesses have participated in adopt-a-school programs, in which a particular company forms a relationship with
a specific school. Sometimes it supplies money for band uniforms
or arranges for special excursions for the students. Typically
there are photo opportunities for the business associated with
the event. Sometimes these programs have been very helpful
in alerting businesspeople to the reality of children's and teachers' lives. Under this plan some companies have provided equipment, typically equipment manufactured by the company, to
the schools. Such plans were the source of closetfuls of overhead
projectors in American schools in the 1960s. Today the equipment is more likely to be computers.

Programs in which company employees become mentors of
schoolchildren, many of whom have too few caring and competent adults in their lives, are another way in which business
has worked with schools. General Electric has developed a program using both current and retired employees, mostly from
middle management, to work with children in schools near GE
plants, such as the Aiken Senior High School in Cincinnati. Jack
Schroder, the principal of Aiken, attributes much of his school's
improvement to the mentors' help.

One example of personal commitment to help youngsters
persevere in their schooling is Eugene Lang's promise of college
support to elementary school students. Lang grew up in Harlem

in the first half of the twentieth century when it was still a melting-pot neighborhood for diverse ethnic groups attempting to become successful in America. When he returned to his elementary school in the last quarter of the twentieth century, he discovered that the "work hard education ethic" he recalled from his childhood no longer prevailed. The community surrounding the school no longer offered the hope or the opportunity he remembered from his youth. In order to provide both, he promised the sixth grade graduating class that he would provide them with college scholarships if they finished high school satisfactorily. He then decided, wisely, that if his program was to have many college students, he would need to provide some ancillary counseling services for the high school students. His program has been widely emulated and undoubtedly will help some students, particularly in its combination of motivational and financial aid. Ten years after its inception only a small number of the students have completed college, and Lang has concluded that many of these students face such serious difficulties that college is not a viable option for them.[29]

Each of the programs I have described is worthy in its own right. And probably activities on this level are a good way to begin if the American business community is to recognize the enormity of the problems that the young present and the importance of young people's healthy development and education for the future of our society. These programs give the adult participants insight into the problems as well as a sense of contributing to their solutions. The adults who take part in them indubitably benefit: not only are they helping children and gaining a better understanding of issues of schooling, but they are also engaging in civic activism, which we value in our society, and they are building new personal relationships.

These partnerships between business and schools are a promising first step in the long road to gain business support for school improvement. They provide concrete forms of assistance and do not force the adults to rely on long-term efforts without immediate indications of results. But adults can also quit these programs when they get discouraged. The daily responsibilities for these activities can be delegated to the human resources or community liaison office and need not involve key members of the company except for occasional ceremonial appearances. These programs can bring good public relations for the company in the community. Showing the CEO with members of the school choir in robes donated by the company is a great photo opportunity.

Symbolically and as a beginning, such individual, local programs are extremely valuable. They will not, however, provide the fundamental change that the nation requires in its schools. They are too dependent on precarious relationships between employees and school people and the children themselves. Neither do they go to the heart of the issue: changing the circumstances of life for many children and changing the expectations and effectiveness of schools. The American system of caring for our young and of educating them needs profound renovation, and these palliatives will not accomplish that. They may, however, set the stage so that fundamental reform becomes more likely.

What is most important about partnerships between business and schools at the local level is that children have a new and powerful advocate both for them and for the schooling they need. This is particularly vital for children in the cities, where until business began to take an interest there were woefully few effective advocates either for children or for education. The school custodians have fared much better than the city children.

Schools have become accustomed to following society's agenda for them. In many wealthy suburban communities, graduates' acceptance to selective colleges has been the litmus test of whether the schools were doing a good job. In other towns the performance of the football or basketball team has been the community index of school performance. Effective external pressures for student achievement from family and community have been missing in recent years for urban public schools, and the school systems have not generated such pressure themselves, although individual teachers and administrators have. The opportunity now is for the business community to exert that pressure within the community for the improvement of children's educations. Business needs to recognize that schools cannot accomplish this task alone but that schools must be strengthened if they are to become more effective. The advocacy must be based on knowledge of the realities of children and schools, and hence the value of these adopt-a-school efforts. It must also be based on a recognition of the need for restructuring, and hence the value of reorganization of the schools and of the retraining of educators. Ultimately, the circumstances of children's lives must be changed, particularly for those in poverty. If intervention by business helps such change to occur, then business will have provided a powerful boost to urban school children and, thus, to the nation.

To conclude, advocacy for children, for their healthy development, for their broad education, for their schools, is a powerful contribution that American business can make, if it chooses, to help our people, our country, and thereby, American business itself. Of the institutions discussed in this book—families, government, higher education—business is uniquely able to make this contribution for children. Not all families, unfortunately, can be effective and powerful advocates for their own children. Those children born into families that cannot or do not serve them well deserve the support and services that effective advocacy brings. Government functions best when advocates push it; the advocacy of higher education has largely been limited to funding for student aid and research, and has certainly not focused on programs for children. The elderly, using their lobbying and voting power, have demonstrated the power of advocacy. Previously they were the poorest segment of our population; now children are. Children by virtue of their age cannot lobby for themselves. Adults must support them, and to date no powerful group of adults has done so. Business can provide that leadership on behalf of children. Without such advocacy for the services they need and to which they are entitled, children will suffer and so will the nation.

· 6 ·

Postscript

One March day a silver-haired General Electric engineer volunteered to judge a science fair at an elementary school in East San Jose, California. He was one of several judges, and the assignment he drew was the kindergarten group. Like many successful engineers, he had long had an interest in science, one that was shared by some of his children, including a daughter who had become a physician. Despite his own and his children's long-term fascination with scientific matters, he was astounded by the quality of the kindergartners' projects, some individual and some group efforts. One little girl had studied seed germination, carefully observing seeds left in her warm garage and others left outside in the chilly winter sun. A group of children studying African animals presented a series of pictures illustrating lions nursing their young and explained that this was the determining characteristic of mammals. The GE engineer concluded that these five-year-olds in their multi-ethnic public school were much further advanced in science than he and his fellow five-year-olds had been in their all-white public school in Idaho half a century before.

The East San Jose kindergarten encapsulates both the promise and the dilemma of American education today: wonderful individual programs and schools exist, but they are not universal. In that kindergarten, Asian, Black, Caucasian, Hispanic, and Native American children are off to a rollicking start in science, but older American schoolchildren trail far behind those of other nations in scientific achievement. Unless we bring about profound changes both in our society's care for children and in our schools' instruction of them, these enthusiastic kindergartners are not likely to maintain their current scientific prowess.

Will their families be able and inclined to support their study? Many of these children do not come from affluent homes. Were they from the fortunate half of families eligible for WIC who got food and health aid, or from the unfortunate half who were eligible but did not get the benefits because funds were not available for them? Were they part of the 22 percent of the children eligible for Head Start who participated in the program, or were they from the 78 percent of eligible children who could not participate because funds were not available for them? Were they among the 48 percent of U.S. four-year-olds or the 29 percent of three-year-olds who participate in an early childhood program? By comparison, almost all French and Belgian children and nearly 90 percent of Italian children are in such programs. These are the youngsters with whom the East San Jose kindergartners will eventually compete on the science tests and later in the world economy.

Will the children's families support them in studying, insisting that they choose a rigorous curriculum that may well demand that they reduce their television watching time or limit their employment during the school year to no more than ten hours per week? When a child does not do well in a given subject, be it mathematics or English or history, will the family excuse the child, saying he or she does not have an aptitude for it, or will the family insist that the child must simply work harder at it? Given the fractured nature of many families and communities today, who are the adults who will play these demanding but crucial roles in the children's lives?

If all our children were healthy, physically and emotionally, and all were supported by their parents and communities to work hard in schools, few changes in schools would be needed. Such children now generally prosper in school. Our first and most important goal should be to create better conditions for all children—to reduce their poverty, improve their health, and provide adult care. One cannot legislate love, which is what all children supremely need and deserve, but American society ought to be able to ensure sustenance, medical support, and adult guidance for all our children.

Recognizing our children's welfare as paramount, then what should we do about our schools? First, our schools need to recognize the circumstances of their students' lives. Recognition need not mean acceptance, as wise and committed educators throughout the nation understand. Realizing that their school is the one outpost of civility and concern in a neighborhood of violence and distrust may mean utilizing the building for much more than simple instruction of the children five hours a day, 180 days a year. The school as a community center is a very old idea, but the need for it is even greater in urban America in the late twentieth century than it was in upstate New York in the late nineteenth or in urban Chicago in the early twentieth. San Diego's New Beginnings, which offers families many social services at the school site, is one such example today.

Schools must establish credibility for their diplomas. If a youngster has a high school diploma, it must mean that he or she has mastered a high school curriculum. Too many holders of such a diploma today have not done so. If a school graduates a student, then employers, colleges, and the American public have a right to expect the student to be able to perform academically. Schools themselves must assume responsibility for assuring the competence of their graduates, and some, such as the ones in Chesapeake, Virginia, are doing just this. There is no single formula for all schools. Some will choose adaptations of James Comer's plan; others may select variations on Theodore Sizer's Coalition of Essential Schools; others will create their own means of assuring that their students learn.

If these changes in organization and pedagogy are to occur, then schools will need support in a variety of forms: money, to send the teachers and administrators to places that can help them with their new tasks, ideally universities and their schools of education but quite possibly other training sites as well; ideas, both to understand the problems the schools face and even more important to determine how to solve them; skills, to negotiate within the community the changes that are necessary; and community backing, to provide advocacy for the children and for the necessity of good education for all. Most of all, the schools need people who will serve the schools and children as teachers and administrators and will be knowledgeable about their fields, skilled in their pedagogy, passionate in their concern for their students, and committed to educating all our children well.

The schools will not flourish, and our children will not be educated, unless the entire nation recognizes and acts to improve the schools and to support the children. The schools cannot do it alone. The crisis is upon us, all of us. We—families, government, higher education, and business—must sustain our schools. Unless we do so, our prospects are dim: our nation weakened, our democracy diminished, and our future limited.

Notes

1. No Golden Age

1. Parts of this chapter first appeared in Patricia Albjerg Graham, "Schools: Cacophony about Practice, Silence about Purpose," *Daedalus* 113, no. 4 (Fall 1984), pp. 29–57; and "Achievement for At-Risk Students," in *School Success for Students at Risk: Analysis and Recommendations of the Council of Chief State School Officers* (Orlando, Fla.: Harcourt Brace Jovanovich, 1988), pp. 154–174.

2. Samuel G. Freedman, *Small Victories: The Real World of a Teacher, Her Students, and Their High School* (New York: Harper and Row, 1990).

3. U.S. National Center for Education Statistics, *Digest of Educational Statistics: 1990* (Washington, D.C.: U.S. Government Printing Office, 1991), pp. 108, 110.

4. Linda Matchan, "Child Triumphs in a Hard, Homeless World," *Boston Globe* (December 23, 1990), pp. 1, 28.

5. G. Stanley Hall, *Adolescence: Its Psychology and Its Relations to Physiology, Anthropology, Sociology, Sex, Crime, Religion, and Education* (New York: D. Appleton, 1904).

6. David A. Hamburg, "Preparing for Life: The Critical Transition of Adolescence," 1988 Annual Report, Carnegie Corporation of New York (New York: Carnegie Corporation, 1988), pp. 3–4.

7. U.S. National Center for Education Statistics, *Digest of Educational Statistics*, p. 108.

8. Urie Bronfenbrenner, *Two Worlds of Childhood: U.S. and U.S.S.R.* (New York: Russell Sage Foundation, 1970).

9. James S. Coleman, *The Adolescent Society* (New York: Free Press, 1961), p. 4.

10. Eleanor Farrar McGowan and David K. Cohen, "Career Education—Reforming School through Work," *Public Interest* 46 (Winter 1977), p. 31.

11. Educational Policies Commission, National Education Association, and American Association of School Administrators, *Education for All American Youth: A Further Look* (Washington, D.C., 1952), p. 3; U.S. National Center for Education Statistics, *Digest of Education Statistics*, p. 108. Rosalind R. Bruno, "School Enrollment—Social and Economic Characteristics of Students: October 1988 and 1987," *Current Population Reports*, Population Characteristics, ser. P–20, no. 443 (1990), p. 12.

12. Charles W. Eliot, "Industrial Education as an Essential Factor in Our National Prosperity," in National Society for the Promotion of Education, *Bulletin* 5 (1908), pp. 12–13.

13. Clarence S. Yoakum and Robert M. Yerkes, *Army Mental Tests* (New York: H. Holt, 1920), p. 189. For a fuller discussion, see Paul Davis Chapman, *Schools as Sorters: Lewis M. Terman, Applied Psychology, and the Intelligence Testing Movement* (New York: New York University Press, 1988).

14. Leonard P. Ayres, *Laggards in Our Schools* (New York: Russell Sage Foundation, 1909), pp. 14–15.

15. Carl C. Brigham, *A Study of American Intelligence* (Princeton, N.J.: Princeton University Press, 1922), pp. 120–121.

16. Thomas Briggs, *The Great Investment, Secondary Education in a Democracy* (Cambridge, Mass.: Harvard University Press, 1930), pp. 120, 124.

17. Arthur Bestor, *Educational Wastelands: The Retreat from Learning in Our Public Schools* (Urbana: University of Illinois Press, 1953); Albert Lynd, *Quackery in the Public Schools* (Boston: Little, Brown, 1950, 1953); Robert M. Hutchins, *The Conflict of Education in a Democratic Society* (New York: Harper and Bros., 1953); Hyman G. Rickover, *Education and Freedom* (New York: E. P. Dutton, 1959).

18. Paul Copperman, *The Literacy Hoax: The Decline of Reading, Writing, and Learning in the Public Schools and What We Can Do about It* (New York: Morrow, 1978); Frank Armbruster, *Our Children's Crippled Future: How American Education Has Failed* (New York: Quadrangle/New York Times Book Company, 1977); National Commission on Excellence in Education, *A Nation at Risk: The Imperative for Educational Reform* (Washington, D.C.: U.S. Government Printing Office, 1983), p. 11.

19. College Entrance Examination Board, Advisory Panel on the Scholastic Aptitude Test Score Decline, Willard Wirtz, Chairman, *On Further Examination: Report Of the Advisory Panel on the Scholastic Aptitude Test Score Decline* (New York: College Entrance Examination Board, 1977).

20. Harold W. Stevenson, Shin-Ying Lee, in collaboration with Chuansheng Chen et al., *Contexts of Achievement: A Study of American, Chinese, and Japanese Children* (Chicago: University of Chicago Press, 1990); Daniel A. Wagner and Harold W. Stevenson, eds., *Cultural Perspectives on Child Development* (San Francisco: W. H. Freeman, 1982).

21. College Entrance Examination Board, *On Further Examination*, pp. 46–48.

22. Roger Farr, Jaap Tuinman, and Michael Rowls, "Reading Achievement in the United States: Then and Now," prepared for Educational Testing Service by the Reading Program Center and the Institute for Child Study, Contract OEC-71-3715 (Bloomington, Ind., 1974), p. 134.

23. Lawrence C. Stedman and Carl F. Kaestle, "An Investigation of Crude Literacy, Reading Performance, and Functional Literacy in the United States, 1880 to 1980," Program Report 86-2 (Madison: Wisconsin Center for Education Research, 1985), pp. 77–78. For a fuller discussion, see Carl F. Kaestle et al., *Literacy in the United States: Readers and Reading Since 1880* (New Haven, Conn.: Yale University Press, 1991).

24. National Commission on Testing and Public Policy, "From Gatekeeper to Gateway: Transforming Testing in America," Report of the National Commission on Testing and Public Policy (Chestnut Hill, Mass.: Boston College, 1990).

25. Dennie Wolf, Janet Bixby, John Glenn III, and Howard Gard-

ner, "To Use Their Minds Well: Investigating New Forms of Student Assessment," in Gerald Grant, ed., *Review of Research in Education* 17 (Washington, D.C.: American Education Research Association, 1991), pp. 31–74; Howard Gardner, "The Difficulties of School: Probable Causes, Possible Cures," *Daedalus* 119 (Spring 1990), pp. 85–113; and "Assessment in Context: The Alternative to Standardized Testing," in Bernard R. Gifford and Mary Catherine O'Connor, eds., *Changing Assessments: Alternative Views of Aptitude, Achievement, and Instruction* (Norwell, Mass.: Kluwer Academic Press, in press); Dennie Palmer Wolf, "Portfolio Assessment: Sampling Student Work," *Educational Leadership* 46 (April 1989), pp. 35–39; and "Opening Up Assessment," *Educational Leadership* 45 (December 1987), pp. 24–29.

26. Lawrence A. Cremin, *Popular Education and Its Discontents* (New York: Harper and Row, 1990), pp. 7–8.

27. Kenneth T. Jackson, *Crabgrass Frontier: The Suburbanization of the United States* (New York: Oxford University Press, 1985).

28. "Tenure of Superintendents," *Education Week* (November 14, 1990), p. 3.

29. Susan Moore Johnson, *Teachers at Work* (New York: Basic Books, 1990), and "Making Schools Work for Teachers," *Harvard Education Letter*, no. 6 (November/December 1990), pp. 1–4.

2. Families

1. Israel Scheffler, "Teachers of My Youth: An American Jewish Experience" (manuscript, Harvard Graduate School of Education, 1987); Sara Lawrence Lightfoot, *Balm in Gilead: Journey of a Healer* (Reading, Mass.: Addison-Wesley, 1988); Sissela Bok, *Alva Myrdal: A Daughter's Memoir* (New York: Addison-Wesley, 1991).

2. Richard Hofstadter, *Anti-Intellectualism in American Life* (New York: Knopf, 1963).

3. Nielsen Media Research (February 1990), in Mark S. Hoffman, ed., *World Almanac and Book of Facts, 1991* (New York: World Almanac/Pharos Books, 1990), p. 317; "What Children Learn from Television," *Harvard Education Letter*, no. 2 (April 1985), pp. 1–6; Blayne Cutler, "Where Does the Free Time Go?" *American Demographics* (November 1990), p. 38.

4. Robert Kubey and Mihaly Csikszentmihalyi, *Television and the Quality of Life: How Viewing Shapes Everyday Experience* (Hillsdale, N.J.: Lawrence Erlbaum Associates, 1990), p. 114.

5. National Center for Children in Poverty, *Five Million Children: A Statistical Profile of Our Poorest Young Citizens* (New York: School of Public Health, Columbia University, 1990), pp. 16, 20.

6. Sandra L. Hofferth and Deborah A. Phillips, "Child Care in the United States, 1970 to 1995," *Journal of Marriage and the Family* 49 (August 1987), p. 560.

7. Claudia Goldin, *Understanding the Gender Gap: An Economic History of American Women* (Oxford: Oxford University Press, 1990), p. 61; Paul Blustein, "Some Swing Group Voters Miss Out on Prosperity," *Washington Post* (September 22, 1988), pp. Al, A29-A30. For a discussion of income distribution in the United States in the post–World War II period see Frank Levy, *Dollars and Dreams: The Changing American Income Distribution* (New York: Norton, 1988). The stagnation of wages and the collapse of productivity growth since 1973 is discussed in Frank Levy and Richard C. Michel, *The Economic Future of American Families: Income and Wealth Trends* (Washington, D.C.: Urban Institute Press, 1991).

8. U.S. Bureau of the Census, "Money Income and Poverty Status in the United States: 1989," *Current Population Reports*, Consumer Income, ser. P-60, no. 168 (September 1990), p. 30.

9. U.S. Bureau of the Census, *Statistical Abstract of the United States: 1990* (Washington, D.C.: U.S. Government Printing Office, 1990), p. 86.

10. U.S. Bureau of the Census, "Marital Status and Living Arrangements: March 1989," *Current Population Reports*, Population Characteristics, ser. P-20, no. 445 (June 1990), p. 3.

11. Deborah L. Cohen, "Parents as Partners: Helping Families Build a Foundation for Learning," *Education Week* (May 9, 1990), p. 14.

12. Louis Harris and Associates, *The Metropolitan Life Survey of the American Teacher, 1987* (New York: Louis Harris and Associates, 1987), p. 21.

13. Robert N. Bellah et al., *Habits of the Heart: Individualism and Commitment in American Life* (Berkeley: University of California Press, 1985).

14. Michael Oreskes, "Today's Youth Cares Less for Worries of the World," *New York Times* (June 28, 1990), p. D21.

15. H. G. Bissinger, *Friday Night Lights: A Town, a Team, and a Dream* (New York: Addison-Wesley, 1990).

16. Sara Lawrence Lightfoot, *Worlds Apart: Relationships between Families and Schools* (New York: Basic Books, 1978). See also Lawrence A. Cremin, *American Education: The Colonial Experience, 1607–1783* (New York: Harper and Row, 1970), *American Education: the National Experience, 1783–1876* (New York: Harper and Row, 1980), *American Education: The Metropolitan Experience, 1876–1980* (New York: Harper and Row, 1988), and *Popular Education and Its Discontents* (New York: Harper and Row, 1990); Harold Howe II, "Reflections on Education and Schooling," in Derek L. Burleson, ed., *Reflections: Personal Essays by Thirty-three Distinguished Educators* (Bloomington, Ind.: Phi Delta Kappa Educational Foundation, 1991), pp. 219–231; Hope Jensen Leichter, ed., *The Family as Educator* (New York: Teachers College Press, 1975), and *Families and Communities as Educators* (New York: Teachers College Press, 1979); Lynn Olson, "Parents as Partners: Redefining the Social Contract between Families and Schools," *Education Week* (April 4, 1990), pp. 17–24; Deborah L. Cohen, "Parents as Partners: Helping Families Build a Foundation for Learning," *Education Week* (May 9, 1990), pp. 13–23.

17. Caroline Farrar Ware, *Greenwich Village, 1920–1930: A Comment on American Civilization in the Post-War Years* (Boston: Houghton Mifflin, 1935), p. 332; Denis Doyle, "Education, Reform and the Economy," *Youth Policy Institute* 1, no. 3 (Winter 1989), p. 73.

18. U.S. Bureau of the Census, *Statistical Abstract of the United States*, p. 637.

19. U.S. National Center for Education Statistics, *Digest of Educational Statistics: 1990* (Washington, D.C.: U.S. Government Printing Office, 1990), p. 10; Deborah L. Cohen, "San Diego Agencies Join to Ensure 'New Beginnings' for Families," *Education Week* (January 23, 1991), pp. 1, 16–19; and "Barriers of Poverty and Bureaucracy Pose Challenges to Service Agencies, Families," *Education Week* (January 23, 1991), pp. 16–17.

20. Lisbeth B. Schorr with Daniel Schorr, *Within Our Reach: Breaking the Cycle of Disadvantage* (New York: Anchor Press/Doubleday, 1988).

21. James P. Comer, *Maggie's American Dream: The Life and Times of a Black Family* (New York: New American Library, 1988); *School Power: Implications of an Intervention Project* (New York: Free Press, 1980); "School-Parent Relationships That Work: An Interview with James Comer," *Harvard Education Letter* 4, no. 6 (November/December 1988), pp. 4–6.

22. John U. Ogbu, "Minority Status and Literacy in Comparative Perspective," *Daedalus* 119, no. 2 (Spring 1990), pp. 141–168; Signithia Fordham and John U. Ogbu, "Black Students' School Success: Coping with the Burden of 'Acting White,' " *Urban Review* 18, no. 3 (1986), pp. 176–206.

23. See Peter L. Buttenweiser, "Unfulfilled Dreams: Thoughts on Progressive Education and the New City Schools, 1900–1978," in Diane Ravitch and Ronald K. Goodenow, eds., *Educating an Urban People: The New York City Experience* (New York: Teachers College Press, 1981), pp. 171–186. For an example of a program for young mothers see Kenneth Worthy, "Teen Mothers Get a Second Chance," *Atlanta Constitution*, Intown Extra (June 8, 1989), p. 5E.

24. Heather B. Weiss, "Nurturing Our Young Children: Building New Partnerships among Families, Schools, and Communities," in *Early Childhood and Family Education: Analysis and Recommendations of the Council of Chief State School Officers* (Orlando, Fla.: Harcourt Brace Jovanovich, 1990).

25. David A. Hamburg, "Early Adolescence: A Critical Time for Interventions in Education and Health" (New York: Carnegie Corporation of New York, 1989); Task Force on Education of Young Adolescents of the Carnegie Council on Adolescent Development, *Turning Points: Preparing American Youth for the 21st Century* (Washington, D.C.: Carnegie Council on Adolescent Development, 1989).

26. Marc Freedman, "Mentoring: New Help for Kids and Schools," *Harvard Education Letter* 7, no. 2 (March/April 1991), pp. 1–3.

27. Eric Zorn, "Many Students Ignoring Their Real Job: School," *Chicago Tribune* (December 18, 1990), section 2, p. 1.

28. Bruce D. Butterfield, "Children at Work: Long Hours, Late Nights, Low Grades," *Boston Globe* (April 24, 1990), p. 12.

29. Ibid.

30. Paul E. Barton, "Earning and Learning: The Academic Achievement of High School Juniors with Jobs," National Assessment

of Educational Progress, Educational Testing Service, Report no. 17–WL-01 (March 1989), pp. 6–7.

31. Ibid., p. 11.

32. Carol Gordon Carlson, "Beyond High School: The Transition to Work," *Focus* 25 (1990), p. 4; "Teenagers Who Work: The Lessons of After-School Employment," *Harvard Educational Letter* 2, no. 5 (September 1986), pp. 1–3.

33. Youth and America's Future: The William T. Grant Foundation Commission on Work, Family and Citizenship, *The Forgotten Half: Non-college Youth in America* (Washington, D.C.: William T. Grant Foundation, 1988); Stephen F. Hamilton, *Apprenticeship for Adulthood: Preparing Youth for the Future* (New York: Free Press, 1990).

3. Government

1. U.S. National Center for Education Statistics, *Digest of Educational Statistics: 1990* (Washington, D.C.: U.S. Government Printing Office, 1991), p. 32; Reagan Walker, "Lawmakers in Ky. Approve Landmark School-Reform Bill," *Education Week* (April 4, 1990), pp. 1, 34–35.

2. Herman B. Leonard, "The Choices Massachusetts Makes: A Comparative Analysis of State and Local Spending, Summary of Approach and Preliminary Results" (John F. Kennedy School of Government, Harvard University, November 1990), p. 3.

3. Michael deCourcy Hinds and Erik Eckholm, "80s Leave States and Cities in Need," *New York Times* (December 30, 1990), p. 17.

4. Edith R. Hornor, *Massachusetts Municipal Profiles, 1990–91* (Palo Alto, Calif.: Information Publications, 1990), pp. 59, 209; Massachusetts Department of Education, Bureau of Data Collection/Processing, "1988–1989 Average Teacher Salary" (February 20, 1989).

5. Marian Wright Edelman, *Families in Peril: An Agenda for Social Change* (Cambridge, Mass.: Harvard University Press, 1987), pp. 39, 47–48.

6. As quoted in Daniel Goleman, "New Measure Finds Growing Hardship for Youth," *New York Times* (October 19, 1989), p. B19.

7. Marian Wright Edelman, "Why America May Go to Hell," *America* (March 31, 1990), p. 311.

8. U.S. House of Representatives, Select Committee on Chil-

dren, Youth, and Families, *U.S. Children and Their Families: Current Conditions and Recent Trends, 1989*, 101st Cong., 1st sess., 1989, pp. 106, 110, 101, 109. See also Sally Reed and R. Craig Sautter, "Children of Poverty: The Status of 12 Million Young Americans," *Phi Delta Kappan* 71, no. 10 (June 1990), pp. K1–K12.

9. Select Committee on Children, Youth, and Families, *U.S. Children and Their Families*, pp. xi, 194. In 1990 Congress expanded Federal Medicaid health insurance so that by the year 2003 all poor children through the age of eighteen will be covered. Ford Foundation Project on Social Welfare and the American Future, *The Common Good: Social Welfare and the American Future* (New York: Ford Foundation, 1989), pp. 14, 28; Renier quoted in David Nyhan, "When Children Are Malnourished," *Boston Globe* (March 14, 1991), p. 21.

10. U.S. House of Representatives, Select Committee on Children, Youth, and Families, *Children's Well-Being: An International Comparison*, 101st Cong., 2nd sess., 1990.

11. David P. Weickart, *Quality Preschool Programs: A Long-Term Social Investment*, Occasional Paper no. 5, Ford Foundation Project on Social Welfare and the American Future (New York: Ford Foundation, 1989), pp. 5–12; John R. Berreuta-Clement et al., *Changed Lives: The Effects of the Perry Preschool Program on Youths through Age 19* (Ypsilanti, Mich.: High/Scope Educational Research Foundation, 1984).

12. "A Battle Won in the Poverty War," *New York Times* (October 31, 1990), p. A24.

13. Hillary Rodham Clinton, "In France, Day Care Is Every Child's Right," *New York Times* (April 7, 1990), p. 25; Fred M. Hechinger, "Why France Outstrips the United States in Nurturing Its Children," *New York Times* (August 1, 1990), p. B8; and Patricia P. Olmstead and David P. Weickart, eds., *How Nations Serve Young Children: Profiles of Child Care and Education in 14 Countries* (Ypsilanti, Mich.: The High/Scope Press, 1989).

14. Donald R. Warren, *To Enforce Education: A History of the Founding Years of the United States Office of Education* (Detroit: Wayne State University Press, 1974), pp. 82, 179; U.S. Office of Management and Budget, *Special Analyses, Budget of the United States Government, Fiscal Year 1980* (Washington, D.C.: U.S. Government Printing Office, 1980), p. 75; Department of Economics and Statistics,

Organization for Economic Co-Operation and Development (OECD), *National Accounts, Main Aggregates, 1960–1988* (Paris: OECD Publications, 1990), p. 127.

15. Stephen K. Bailey and Edith K. Mosher, *ESEA: The Office of Education Administers a Law* (Syracuse, N.Y.: Syracuse University Press, 1968), p. viii.

16. U.S. Accounting Office, *Education Information: Changes in Funds and Priorities Have Affected Production and Quality* (Washington, D.C.: General Accounting Office, 1987), p. 69.

17. Kearns quoted in Edward B. Fiske, "Lessons/Educational Research: Short on Resources, Quality and Impact," *New York Times* (August 23, 1989), p. B8.

18. U.S. Office of Management and Budget, *Budget of the United States Government, Fiscal Year 1992* (Washington, D.C.: U.S. Government Printing Office, 1991), pt. 4, pp. 66–67, 91, 589.

19. Ibid., pp. 590, 1124. "Flashcard," *New York Times* (August 5, 1990), section 4A, p. 12.

20. FCCSET Committee on Education and Human Resources, "By the Year 2000: First in the World" (February 1991), p. 27; "Administration FY 92 Budget Request to Maintain Federal Arts Funding at $174 Million," *National Endowment for the Arts News* (February 4, 1991), p. 2; "National Endowment for the Humanities: Summary of Requested Appropriations for Fiscal Year 1992," *Facts* (1991), p. 9.

21. Barbara Gamarekian, "Ads Aimed at Children Restricted," *New York Times* (October 18, 1990), pp. D1–D2; and Jeremy Gerard, "House Passes Bill to Restrict Ads on Children's Television Programs," *New York Times* (July 24, 1990), p. A16.

22. National Commission on Excellence in Education, *A Nation at Risk: The Imperative for Educational Reform* (Washington, D.C.: U.S. Government Printing Office, 1983); U.S. Department of Education, *America 2000: An Education Strategy* (Washington, D.C.: U.S. Government Printing Office, 1991).

23. U.S. Department of Education, *America 2000*, p. 9.

24. U.S. National Center for Education Statistics, *Digest of Educational Statistics*, p. 34.

25. "Final Education Department Budget for Fiscal 1991," *Education Week* (November 7, 1990), pp. 20–21.

4. Higher Education

1. Parts of this chapter were presented in the Louise McBee Lecture at the University of Georgia on October 5, 1989, and were published as Patricia Albjerg Graham, "Collaborating for Children and Schools: The Role of Higher Education" (Athens, Ga.: Institute of Higher Education, 1990).

2. U.S. National Center for Education Statistics, *Digest of Educational Statistics: 1990* (Washington, D.C.: U.S. Government Printing Office, 1991), p. 170.

3. Ibid., p. 219. Effie H. Jones and Xenia P. Montenegro, *Women and Minorities in School Administration* (Arlington, Va.: American Association of School Administrators, 1988), p. 13; Madeleine F. Green, *The American College President: A Contemporary Profile* (Washington, D.C.: American Council on Education, 1988), p. 4.

4. Susan Dodge, "Average Score on Verbal Section of '89-'90 SAT Drops to Lowest Level Since 1980; Math Score Unchanged," *Chronicle of Higher Education* (September 5, 1990), p. A33.

5. Samuel Weiss, "CUNY Trustees Vote to Adopt New Standards," *New York Times* (February 26, 1991), pp. A1, A2; and "CUNY Standards Would Press Schools," *New York Times* (January 24, 1991), pp. B1, B2.

6. Richard J. Light, "The Harvard Assessment Seminars: Explorations with Students and Faculty about Teaching, Learning, and Student Life," First Report (Cambridge, Mass.: Harvard University Graduate School of Education and Kennedy School of Government, 1990).

7. Donald A. Schon, *The Reflective Practitioner: How Professionals Think in Action* (New York: Basic Books, 1983).

8. Donald A. Schon, *Educating the Reflective Practitioner: Toward a New Design for Teaching and Learning the Professions* (San Francisco: Jossey-Bass, 1987).

9. Arthur G. Powell, *The Uncertain Profession: Harvard and the Search for Educational Authority* (Cambridge, Mass.: Harvard University Press, 1980), p. 176.

10. Geraldine Joncich Clifford and James W. Guthrie, *Ed School: A Brief for Professional Education* (Chicago: University of Chicago Press, 1988). See especially ch. 6, "Case Studies in Academic Politics

and Institutional Cultures," pp. 202–257, for accounts of the difficulties at Yale, Duke, Chicago, and Michigan.

11. "A Peace Corps for America," *Boston Globe* (June 8, 1990), p. 16, and Michael Marriot, "For Fledgling Teacher Corps, Hard Lessons," *New York Times* (December 5, 1990), pp. A1, B15.

12. These two prototypes are described in Harry G. Judge, *American Graduate Schools of Education: A View from Abroad* (New York: Ford Foundation, 1982). Many of the same issues are addressed in Clifford and Guthrie, *Ed School*.

5. Business

1. Jorie W. Philippi, "Facilitating the Flow of Information between the Business and Education Communities," in Commission on Workforce Quality and Labor Market Efficiency, *Investing in People: A Strategy to Address America's Workforce Crisis* (Washington, D.C.: U.S. Department of Labor, 1989), p. 704. These statistics are not from any large-scale research project, but rather are derived from personal communications between Philippi and McDonalds Triangle Horseshoe Mfg., South Carolina; Walgreen Company, Illinois; and the American Bankers Association and its affiliates. However, these statistics may be indicative of the problem.

2. Susan Chira, "Trying to Coax a Work Force from the Schools of New York," *New York Times* (July 30, 1989), p. E5.

3. Ford Foundation Project on Social Welfare and the American Future, *The Common Good: Social Welfare and the American Future* (New York: Ford Foundation, 1989), p. 33.

4. Russell W. Rumberger and Henry M. Levin, "Schooling for the Modern Workplace," in Commission on Workforce Quality and Labor Market Efficiency, *Investing in People*, p. 108. See also Ina V. S. Mullis, Eugene H. Owen, and Gary W. Phillips, *America's Challenge: Accelerating Academic Achievement, A Summary of Findings from 20 Years of NAEP* (Princeton, N.J.: Educational Testing Service, 1990), pp. 38–53.

5. Barbara Rogoff and Jean Lave, eds., *Everyday Cognition: Its Development in Social Context* (Cambridge, Mass.: Harvard University Press, 1984); Lauren Resnick, *Education and Learning to Think* (Washington, D.C.: National Academy Press, 1987); Howard Gardner, "As-

sessment in Context: The Alternative to Standardized Testing," in Bernard R. Gifford and Mary Catherine O'Connor, eds., *Changing Assessments: Alternative Views of Aptitude, Achievement, and Instruction* (Norwell, Mass.: Kluwer Academic Press, in press).

6. Elizabeth M. Fowler, "An Emphasis on Training for the 1990s," *New York Times* (December 25, 1990), p. 47; Patricia Wallace, "Colleges Should Develop New Ways to Meet the Training Needs of Business," *Chronicle of Higher Education* (December 16, 1990), p. A36. For a thorough discussion of adult training in the workplace see Nell P. Eurich, *The Learning Industry: Education for Adult Workers* (Princeton, N.J.: Carnegie Foundation for the Advancement of Teaching, 1990).

7. Christopher M. Harris, "Conflict and Educational Reform: The Experience of Mississippi, Pennsylvania, and West Virginia" (Ed.D. diss., Harvard Graduate School of Education, 1990).

8. As quoted in Steven A. Holmes, "House Backs Bush Veto of Family Leave Bill," *New York Times* (July 26, 1990), p. A16.

9. Cited in Carol Gordon Carlson, "Beyond High School: The Transition to Work," *Focus* 25 (1990), p. 4.

10. Research and Policy Committee of the Committee for Economic Development, *The Unfinished Agenda: A New Vision for Child Development and Education* (New York: Committee on Economic Development, 1991), p. 47.

11. "How Well Are Schools Performing? Educators, Executives Don't Agree," *Education Week* (February 14, 1990), p. 11.

12. Nell P. Eurich, *Corporate Classrooms: The Learning Business* (Princeton, N.J.: Carnegie Foundation for the Advancement of Teaching, 1985). William Wiggenhorn, "Motorola U: When Training Becomes an Education," *Harvard Business Review* (July-August, 1990), pp. 317–329.

13. Richard J. Murnane, "Education and the Productivity of the Work Force: Looking Ahead," in Robert E. Litan, Robert Z. Lawrence, and Charles L. Schultze, eds., *American Living Standards: Threats and Challenges* (Washington, D.C.: Brookings Institution, 1988), p. 218.

14. Ibid., p. 221.

15. George S. Counts, *The Social Composition of Boards of Education: A Study in Social Control of Public Education* (Chicago: University of Chicago Press, 1927).

16. David T. Kearns and Denis P. Doyle, *Winning the Brain Race: A Bold Plan to Make Our Schools Competitive* (San Francisco: ICS Press, 1988).

17. Reagan Walker, "Centers to Expand Linkage between Businesses, Schools," *Education Week* (April 18, 1990), p. 1, 20. See also Jeanne Amster, Ernest L. Boyer, and Judy S. Brown, *Investing in Our Future: The Imperatives of Education Reform and the Role of Business* (Queenstown, Md.: Aspen Institute, 1990); R. Scott Fosler, *The Business Role in State Education Reform* (New York: Business Roundtable, 1990); National Alliance of Business, *The Business Roundtable Participation Guide* (New York: Business Roundtable, 1990).

18. Michael L. Dertouzos, Richard K. Lester, and Robert M. Solow, *Made in America: Regaining the Productive Edge* (Cambridge, Mass.: MIT Press, 1989), p. 152.

19. Committee for Economic Development, *CED & Education: National Impact and Next Steps*, A CED Symposium, Annual Meeting of the Trustees, New York, N.Y., 1988, pp. 8–9.

20. U.S. House of Representatives, Select Committee on Children, Youth, and Families, *Children's Well-Being: An International Comparison*, 101st Cong., 2nd sess., 1990, pp. 42, 98, 33.

21. Research and Policy Committee of the Committee for Economic Development, *Investing in Our Children: Business and the Public Schools* (New York: Committee for Economic Development, 1985); *Children in Need: Investment Strategies for the Educationally Disadvantaged* (New York: Committee for Economic Development, 1987); and *The Unfinished Agenda*. See also P. Michael Timpane and Laurie Miller McNeil, *Business Impact on Education and Child Development* (New York: Committee for Economic Development, 1991).

22. Arthur Powell, Eleanor Farrar, and David Cohen, *The Shopping Mall High School: Winners and Losers in the Educational Marketplace* (Boston: Houghton Mifflin, 1985).

23. Raymond E. Callahan, *Education and the Cult of Efficiency* (Chicago: University of Chicago Press, 1962).

24. Richard F. Elmore and Milbrey Wallin McLaughlin, *Steady Work: Policy, Practice, and the Reform of American Education* (Santa Monica, Calif.: Rand Corporation, 1988).

25. Nadine Brozan, "From Citibank, Millions for Schools," *New York Times* (May 16, 1990), p. B7.

26. Dertouzos, Lester, and Solow, *Made in America*, p. 118.

27. Select Committee on Children, Youth, and Families, *Children's Well-Being*, p. 12.

28. Jonathan Weisman, "Major School-Business Pact Launched in Philadelphia," *Education Week* (January 16, 1991), p. 5.

29. Evelyn Nieves, "The Carrot Was Money for College, but Not All Went for It," *New York Times* (July 12, 1991), pp. B1–B2. For an overview and evaluation of private sector tuition-guarantee programs, see U.S. General Accounting Office, "Promising Practice: Private Programs Guaranteeing Student Aid for Higher Education," Report to the Chairman, U.S. Senate Committee on Labor and Human Resources, GAO/PEMD–90–16 (Washington, D.C.: June 1990).

Index

370.973   Graham, Patricia
G   Albjerg.

S.O.S.

BAKER & TAYLOR BOOKS